TORVILL & DEAN

Athletic, balletic, gymnastic, melodic—on so many levels have Jayne Torvill and Christopher Dean rightfully earned themselves a very special place in the hearts of the British public. With their interpretive flair and technical brilliance, they have brought the sport of ice dancing to a new peak of excellence, and focused the world's attention on its exquisite grace, excitement and beauty.

This lively and absorbing biography tells the complete story of their meteoric rise to fame. How sheer hard work and determination won them their first World Championship in 1981 and they then went on to set dazzling new standards with their interpretations of Mack & Mabel (1982), Barnum on Ice (1983), and their latest, hypnotic Bolero (1984) which has won them the 1984 European Championship and that much-coveted Olympic gold medal in Sarajevo.

Yet for all their many triumphs, Torvill and Dean have never let success go to their heads. Biographer John Hennessy—former sports editor of The Times—shows them as they really are: quiet, unassuming young people with a tremendous talent that has taken them all the way to the top, from world-famous sports arenas to receptions at 10 Downing Street and Buckingham Palace.

And what of their own relationship together? In exclusive articles written specially for this book, the two young skaters talk frankly about their lives both on and off the ice, and how they feel about each other behind the scenes.

The first edition, in hardback, was in the bestseller lists for months and this up-to-the-minute, delightful and exciting book is certain to give tremendous pleasure to everyone who loves the athletic grace and beauty of Britain's twin champions, Torvill and Dean.

TORVILL & DEAN

Jayne Torvill and Christopher Dean
with John Hennessy

DAVID & CHARLES
Newton Abbot London

To Betty

the 'great lady'

Frontispiece
An intimate moment, shared by a packed Helsinki arena, as Chris and Jayne leave
the ice to be greeted by a full house of nine 6.0s for their artistic impression of
Barnum, a world record (*All-Sport Photographic*)

British Library Cataloguing in Publication Data
Hennessy, John
    Torvill & Dean.
    1. Torvill, Jayne   2. Dean, Christopher
    3. Skaters—Great Britain—Biography
    I. Title   II. Torvill, Jayne   III. Dean, Christopher
    796.91′092′2   GV850.T/
    ISBN 0-7153-8622-0

© Text: John Hennessy 1984

All rights reserved. No part of this
publication may be reproduced, stored in
a retrieval system, or transmitted, in
any form or by any means, electronic,
mechanical, photocopying, recording or
otherwise, without the prior permission
of David & Charles (Publishers) Limited

Filmset by MS Filmsetting Ltd, Frome, Somerset
and printed in Great Britain
by Butler and Tanner Ltd, Frome, Somerset
for David & Charles (Publishers) Limited
Brunel House, Newton Abbot, Devon

Published in the United States of America
by David & Charles Inc
North Pomfret, Vermont 05053, USA

Contents

Olympic Gold

Christopher Dean squeezed the hand of the girl at his side. She turned, flashed him a lovely smile, and squeezed back. It was something they had never done before in nine years of skating together, but then the experience that faced Christopher and Jayne Torvill was something they had never known before. Within five minutes they were to fulfill a burning personal ambition and, at the same time, answer the yearning of a nation. The Olympic gold medals for ice dance were at stake out there in the snowy wastes of Sarajevo, until now only known to most Britons as the city where two shots rang out in 1914 to signal the start of the First World War.

They glided to the spot on the ice where Chris had earlier scuffed the surface during the warm-up to give them a sure hold as they knelt on their right knees. The applause that had greeted them died away to an expectant hush. Face to face now, they waited the opening strains of *Bolero*. Four minutes and twenty-eight seconds later Ravel's masterpiece of orchestration, scored and recorded specially for them, came to a tumultuous crescendo.

They remember nothing in between. Before a capacity audience who had paid the equivalent of £27—or perhaps more to the ticket touts plying their dubious trade in the biting cold outside the Zetra Stadium—they played out an exquisite scenario conceived by themselves to choreography developed by themselves.

The streets back home, we heard, were emptying as Britain sought a vantage point in front of millions of television sets. A self-imposed curfew took effect in the City of Nottingham, whose heart beat with a special pride, for nowhere were these two young sweethearts of British sport, she twenty-six, he a year younger, held in higher regard. It was a breathless moment, captivating even those hard cases from Fleet Street who had never before attended an ice skating event and been flown out specially to see what all the fuss was about.

From those kneeling positions, symbolically pledging themselves to each other, they swayed around hypnotically to set the tone of the performance. This was a time of personal communion, a time when they played not to the audience but to each other, but the magical atmosphere they created reached out in a way no deliberate posturing could possibly have achieved. The following day, Chris leans back in a chair in the press room of the Olympic village, sighs and searches for an explanation:

The exquisite artistry of Chris and Jayne's spellbinding interpretation of Ravel's *Bolero* was rewarded by maximum marks of nine 6.0s for artistic impression (*Bob Martin/Creative Sport*)

6 It was something we'd waited for and worked for over four long years and I'd counted off the final months. The night before I'd said to myself 'twenty-four hours' and when I woke up it was 'twelve hours'. I was actually counting off the hours now. It was St Valentine's Day and I gave Jayne an orchid. She gave me a kiss. When, at long last, we knelt down on the ice we looked into each other's eyes and saw total commitment. We had felt a coming together through the day and now we were alone out there, just the two of us. It was almost as if we were looking into each other's soul. I can think of only one comparable occasion, when we did the 'Summertime' blues two seasons ago, specially in the European championships in Lyons. We gave one hundred per cent then, or so we thought at the time. In that case this was two hundred per cent. Every time we came face to face during the dance our eyes locked in a sort of oneness. And at the end, when we collapsed in the volcano of our imagination I felt I could have stayed there for ever. Didn't you, Jayne? 9

Jayne nods soulful agreement, and gives her version:

❛ I think we were in a kind of trance and the skating looked after itself. I remember the steps, of course, but were they last night's steps or those of so many practice runs we'd done? If we'd had a little trip or something, that would stick in my mind but all there was were two bursts of clapping, first when Chris did the splits—so unusual for the man to do—and later when he lifted me with his free leg, two things we'd brought into the programme since Budapest. For a moment or two I couldn't hear the music. ❜

Chris tries again:

❛ Sometimes you can think about the blades and your feet, but not last night. It was like someone putting you to sleep under hypnosis and you say things that you've no knowledge of when you're back to normal. At the end we were woken up, if you like, by the end of the music, followed by what seemed to be ecstatic applause. There's a chemistry between us that even we can't understand. I'm sure that neither of us could do what we do with any other partner, could we, Jayne? What's the chance of somebody else coming along with the same temperament, the right age, in the right place and at the right time? ❜

Slowly, reluctantly, they rose from their volcano, took a long bow and collected the floral tributes, some from a party of daytrippers from Nottingham conspicuously wearing Union Jack bowler hats. They did not catch the first set of marks, including three 6.0s; then, Jayne recalls, 'everyone screamed, we looked up and saw nine 6.0s as we had done in Helsinki a year earlier for *Barnum*'.

For those of us in the spellbound audience, there was a chemistry not only between themselves but between themselves and us. Quite early on Chris did his splits, which must have come out of the blue to many spectators denied a sneak preview during practice. They had contemplated doing the move in unison but Jayne had found difficulty in recovering to an upright position. 'You have to be very strong here, on the inside of the thigh,' she says, 'to bring it off.' The impact was still strong, because although splits is a common device in ice dancing, it is nearly always done by the girl partner. Certainly, I cannot recall ever seeing a man do it.

There was now a lyrical swing in their skating. There was never a sign of fallibility as they moved exquisitely from one highlight to the next, timed to coincide with the rising crescendo of Ravel's music.

A particularly proud moment for Chris as he leads the British team in the opening ceremony of the 1984 Winter Olympics at Sarajevo (*Steve Powell/All-Sport Photographic*)

Supreme! British, European, World and now Olympic champions (*Steve Powell/All-Sport Photographic*)

Jayne now climbed to the top of her imaginary volcano with the help of her partner's hand under her boot and an expertise that will have escaped the notice of the uninformed. 'It's a hard take-off,' Chris says. 'She has to do a turn with her leg up. That's the most difficult part, turning from forward inside edge through a complete rotation on one foot with me holding the other leg and then being in line for the take-off. If she's not in line I can't hold her. That takes some skating.' The landing is liable to jar her right up to the hip if incorrectly performed, but this time she came down as soft as a snowflake. The flip over Chris's shoulder was timed to the second and one noticed all too soon that we were nearing the end. The time had flown when Chris went down on one knee for the final spectacular turn—it had brought him down in one practice in a welter of publicity during the week—and it was time to consummate their terrible suicide pact. If the lovers could not be together in life they would be together eternally in the bowl of that smouldering volcano. Chris swung Jayne round and two changes of position of her shoulders were accompanied by a frenzied convulsion on her part. Their moment had come and they died a tragic yet beautiful death.

On the podium for the medal ceremony they were joined by two Russian couples, Natalya Bestemianova and Andrei Bukin, who had escaped from the world champions' monumental shadow only when Jayne's injury forced her and Chris out of the European championship in 1983, and the seventeen-year-old Marina Klimova and Sergei Ponomarenko, who had surprisingly overtaken the American champions, Judy Blumberg and Michael Seibert. Neither could remember any surge of emotion but avid Torvill-Dean watchers, glued to their television screens, detected a struggle to hold back the tears, certainly in Chris's case. Jayne remembered a lighter aspect:

❢ I was amused by the anthem. It was a bit oom-pa-pa—not like in Helsinki where they had a live orchestra. Perhaps we should have brought the Grenadiers out. The President of the International Olympic Committee presented the medals and I couldn't this time resist looking down at mine. Normally you stand there and you don't touch the medal. Chris did the same. You just can't appreciate what those medals mean to us. ❡

For Chris this was the end of a long road:

❢ When we got the Nottingham City grant for the first world championships in 1981 we said the Olympics would have to be our big target. That was the spur. It was nice the first year when we won the worlds, then the second time and the third. Then we were thinking about the next year and Sarajevo. Could we do it, would it come? Anything could happen on the night, so there had to be a lingering doubt. Anybody who doesn't have some fear isn't natural. We tried to protect ourselves, like treading carefully in the icy streets, but it's mainly a case of not catching colds. That usually happens to me, but I escaped this time. Only the day after the competition finished did I begin to feel thick in the throat. **9**

He takes a special pride in *Bolero*:

6 This was the most satisfying thing we've ever done. Right from the start we'd believed in it and felt very confident with it, specially after the changes we'd made during the few weeks between Budapest and Sarajevo. It was already technically very difficult, but we felt it was stronger now. And whereas Budapest was like a try-out, with everybody scrutinizing not only *Bolero* and the original set pattern (OSP) paso doble but also the compulsory dances, there was none of that in Sarajevo, not a word. The small changes we'd made in the compulsory paso doble and Westminster waltz killed off all criticism. Some people may have got hold of the wrong end of the stick about *Bolero*. We didn't think we'd do *Bolero* because we were world champions and reckoned we could get away with something. We did it because that was our interpretation of the free dance this year. And although it was a single rhythm, no-one seemed to notice that with our recording there was nearly a twenty per cent increase in tempo spread across the whole piece. **9**

In total they recorded nineteen marks of 6.0 in Sarajevo to bring their total in all forms of competition to a remarkable 107. There would have been twenty had the referee been able to express an opinion. He was Lawrence Demmy, sitting in that position with all the authority of Chairman of the Ice Dance Committee of the International Skating Union (ISU). A former world champion for Britain, he had been so nervous that he had borrowed a piece of chewing gum to help relieve the tension, never having chewed gum before. He would have broken another habit of a lifetime, he confessed afterwards, with a second mark of 6.0 for artistic impression, had he been able to show his hand. Nineteen 6.0s represented a new milestone for Chris and Jayne, surpassing their seventeen in the European championships in Budapest a month earlier and in Lyons two years earlier.

Their reactions to Sarajevo were in marked contrast to those after their three world championships. Jayne again:

Natalya Bestemianova and Andrei Bukin, perennial runners-up to Chris and Jayne except at Dortmund in 1983 when an injury to Jayne allowed the Russians to take the European title (*Ice & Roller Skate Magazine*)

❛ Usually we feel flat afterwards, because it's the end of the season. It was still a lovely feeling this morning [the day after] because the people around us were so excited. There was a great team spirit among the Brits this time and they were riding with us, full of beans after the party with Princess Anne the night before. Also we've been kept pretty busy in various ways, and there's another championship to go yet. I think that'll be another experience in itself. Our last skate together in competition is bound to be quite emotional, I should imagine. ❜

I asked them, the day after, if they felt closer together as a result of *Bolero*. 'Yes', they both softly answered, but Jayne ruined the romantic mood I had hoped to establish by adding with a giggle 'because he's my friend, a bigger friend than he was yesterday, because he didn't fall down or anything.' Yet an Associated Press picture, circulated world wide, carries extraordinary sexual power in a moment from *Bolero*. Jayne's face is cupped in Chris's hands, their lips no more than half-an-inch apart. Her head and arms are drawn submissively back and from top to toe she presents a sinuous curve of melting surrender. The enigma of their personal relationship deepens.

They had a long St Valentine's Day, with a practice in the afternoon which, Jayne says, served its modest purpose:

❝ We used it to go over the mechanics of the programme rather than skate it properly. In our minds we didn't want to give everything. We could only do that once in a day and we were saving it all for the evening. We could have gone to rest and sleep after lunch but we'd had a lazy morning with just that one practice and we didn't want to get drowsy. We relaxed by watching television, mostly the men's competition short programme. ❞

For Chris:

❝ It was a really long week, not just one day. In the normal way you arrive at a championship for three days of practice and three successive days of competition, boom-boom-boom but, arriving five days before the compulsories, there was too much time to eat up. Some of the practices were getting not exactly lax, but little things were creeping in that you would expect to eliminate in training. At a championship it's like a performance every time, with the judges and the press around.

The worse thing on the day was getting ready to go to the rink. You're by yourself now thinking about the skating. You're doing your hair, you're washing yourself. You're suddenly all alone and all you've got for company are your thoughts and the splash of running water. When we got to the rink this time I had to do quite a long warm-up because of the splits. I have to get my legs going and if I don't do it properly I am likely to do myself an injury. It takes a good thirty minutes. Yet in one way it's a help because it gives me something to do, something to occupy my mind. ❞

Meanwhile Jayne was warming up by herself in her tracksuit and finishing her make-up. There was a time when Chris had to suffer that 'yukky' ordeal, as he called it, if they were skating under bright lights for television, but tanning cream had now replaced the blush of rouge. As the other skaters came and went, we in the stadium knew that the prospects had grown brighter for Chris and Jayne. Natalya Bestemianova, their principal challenger from the Soviet Union at the side of Andrei Bukin, had an attack of nerves and, since she is two-thirds of the partnership with her firecracker personality, their marks were disappointing—for them, that is. They averaged exactly 5.8 and British well-wishers breathed a little more freely; even if Chris and Jayne made a mistake now, they could still expect to improve on those marks—not that that is the way they would want to win an Olympic title. Only a general collapse of morale could now stand in their way, and if there was a craven heart or two that harboured that base suspicion, they were to be gloriously confounded.

Out of our sight they stood at the bottom of a flight of stairs as Karen Barber and Nicky Slater, Britain's second couple, performed their last rituals. Jayne, normally so serene, is the one now who cannot wait to get going while Chris, the more dynamic of the two, is the one who has to apply a restraining hand.

Eventually they appeared in those striking creations of Courtney Jones, wearing his other hat. Chris looked like someone out of Greek mythology with his heroically blond hair and billowing blouse. Jayne appropriately wore a dress inspired by the Greek chiton in matching colours of lilac shading to purple. The colour scheme had sprung from the pretty picture presented by Jayne in her lilac ski-suit on a visit to Jones's flat in London. After the original design was completed, Jones kept tinkering with the outfits— particularly Jayne's—right up to and after the European championships in Budapest. One dark night in Nottingham he had pursued them on the rink, paint pot in hand, to strengthen the colour of the pleats in Chris's blouse. With scissors in hand, he then attacked Jayne's dress with a kind of calculated abandon. He kept slashing bits off here and there as the fancy took him. A regular hemline would be out of place for the tragic scene they were about to enact. The garment is essentially designed for movement. 'When I put it on, before I go on the ice,' Jayne says, 'I'm always fiddling with it, because it never looks right. Then I just forget it.' In motion, it has a dreamlike quality that fits the part perfectly.

They were ready now, waiting to be summoned on the public address, but still they were not allowed to put blade to ice. A tiny tot with outsize boots appeared and skated in her own good time to the far end of the rink, arms decorously held outstretched, to recover something from the ice. Ever alert for omens, we wondered if this charming interlude, so much appreciated by the spectators, might have unnerved Chris and Jayne but 'if anything, it was a little bit of light relief', according to Chris. Their names were called and off they skated, into the hearts of a nation.

The earlier stages of the competition had followed an unexpected course, the compulsories exceeding expectations and the OSP paso doble falling a little flat. Chris:

❝ The crucial thing was the adjustment to the Zetra rink. All week we'd been practising in the smaller rink and it was only on the morning of the paso, at 6.45am, that we had a practice in the main rink. The paso is a barrier dance, like a compulsory, so the position of the barrier is more important than in the free. Now, on the day we had to skate, we weren't familiar with it. It wasn't a brilliant practice. For one thing it was too early in the morning, the music was awful and the man at the controls had to keep turning the sound up and down.　**❜**

There was an unexpected blemish in the OSP which had been a brilliant success in both Nottingham and Budapest. Jayne:

❻ In the flipover I was lower than I would normally be when I twisted, leaning out more, and my hand touched the ice. I don't think we were quite in line. We didn't get the crowd reaction as in Budapest but that didn't worry me. I don't think they understood what we were doing. When we came off we didn't feel flat, because we had the impression that it was still a hockey crowd left over from the night before—an audience of bits and pieces. With due respect, they weren't all skaters and they were only shouting for their own people. We would probably have got a better atmosphere if the place had been full of Yugoslavs who'd wanted to pay and watch, and it had been held in the evening.　**❜**

We must not exaggerate the disappointment of the paso. They still harvested the 6.0s, even two from the Hungarian judge. The Italian and Canadian also gave them 6.0 for the second mark (presentation). The other marks were 5.9. Perhaps, they thought, they would be able to repair that little blow to their pride in the world championships in Ottawa a few weeks later. If there was a flaw in their skating—caused, Chris suggested, by an excess of zeal on his part in order to make an impact on their third sequence—there would surely have been a crop of 6.0s for Jones's design of Jayne's cape, with a glitter of golden embroidery running from fingertip to fingertip across her shoulders.

By way of compensation for that small setback Chris and Jayne had stormed new barriers in the compulsories, with three 6.0s for their Westminster waltz. They had broken their duck in this area with a maximum mark for their rumba in the British championship the previous November, but this was infinitely more satisfying under the scrutiny of an international panel. One of the three was Courtney Jones and 'it was nice', Jayne declares, 'that two other nations joined him'. So far as records immediately available show, there may have been one or two previous instances of a maximum mark in a compulsory in national competitions but this was the first time in an international event—and well deserved. It was a beautiful waltz, with a lovely lilt and swing in marvellous unison. They abandoned the unconventional in the paso which had apparently

Stunning outfits and a dramatic programme for the OSP paso doble set Chris and Jayne well on the road to gold

offended two judges in Budapest. It had the added advantage of giving more drive and swing to the cross rolls, a serpentine feature of the dance. Similarly they had made a fractional change of position in the Westminster waltz to forestall criticism.

All this was fascinating enough at the time, but we now look on it as a series of warm-up acts for that stupendous night when two young people—with a degree of intuitive rapport they do not fully understand themselves—reached out and brought an echo of Henry V's 'and gentlemen in England now a-bed shall think themselves accursed they were not here'.

Under the microscope

The adulation this personable young couple now receive, something akin to royalty in tracksuits, seems so far removed from their origins and the ambitions that might reasonably have been held for their future as to challenge the theory of heredity. Both were born of humble urban stock in the Nottingham City suburbs, the daughter of a bicycle machine operator and the son of a National Coal Board electrician. In neither family was there any previously known skating skill or artistic leaning, nothing in the genes apparently to explain a talent that has captivated a whole nation.

Their introduction to the sport was typical of countless others in Britain and they could so easily have drifted into the hurly-burly seen on any rink on any day of the week, particularly during school holidays. Jayne first attended the Nottingham ice rink with a school party and had no more privileged opportunity than the hundreds of others who experience skating for the first time in this environment. Chris was tempted by the arrival of a pair of skates as a Christmas present after he had tested the ice a time or two. Where they differed from others was in the seriousness of their approach at an early age, a characteristic that still separates them from the rest. They were both about ten and it would be a few years yet before they became conscious of the other's existence. Chris once crashed into a barrier and came home with a broken leg and undiminished enthusiasm.

To begin with, they advanced in different directions. Jayne followed the orthodox experience of school figures which carried her towards solo skating and pairs. Chris from the first veered naturally towards ice dance and never suffered the cold grind of compulsory figures—that drudgery of tracing circles and loops with geometrical embellishments for the more advanced. The paragraphs and brackets, the axel and salchow that are the stock in trade of the figure skater were a mystery to him and would remain so. Even at that tender age Chris was too independently minded to show interest, whereas Jayne tended, and still does under Chris's dynamic inspiration, to be more open to persuasion.

Jayne was the first to achieve national recognition by winning the British junior pairs title with another Nottingham skater, Michael Hutchinson, at the age of twelve under the guidance of Thelma Perry. Later that year they were second in the seniors event and succeeded to that title in 1971. Born on 7 October 1957, she was fourteen at the time. Chris had to bide his time—ice dancers are

Betty Callaway's 'children' in the days when they conventionally filled that role, independently on holiday and unaware of the other's existence.

slower to mature than figure skaters. In the early days, too, he was not the technical equal of Jayne, since he had not gone to school on the figures. Again, Jayne's small physique, particularly at that age, made her an ideal pairs partner. There was not much of her to lift and throw. She and Michael Hutchinson were deposed the following year and Hutchinson went to London in pursuit of another partner and companionship off the ice. Jayne carried on as a solo skater for three more years before time and Christopher Dean caught up with her.

Chris had first made his mark by winning the British primary ice dance championship with Sandra Elson, a friend of Jayne's, in 1972. He was thirteen at the time, born on 27 July 1958. The junior title followed two years later but, for all its early success, it was not likely to prove a fruitful partnership because of friction on the ice. Given his dominating personality nowadays, it is hard to think that Chris could have been overshadowed by any partner, but that was the situation between him and Sandra Elson. His physical equal, she was the boss and it was she who decided to go off in search of a new partner the following spring. How fascinating to recall that the greatest combination that ice skating has known was dependent on both parties being discarded by their previous partners, though admittedly in Chris's case she merely beat him to the draw. Chris and Jayne were now ready to join forces.

The credit for matching these two different talents in 1975 belongs to Janet Sawbridge, who had been British ice dance champion three times between 1963 and 1971 with two different partners. She was a uniquely gifted all-round skater, chosen for both the women's and ice dance events of the European championships in 1965, though she decided to concentrate all her efforts on ice dancing with David Hickinbottom. Chris takes up the story:

‘Our trainer at the time, Len Sayward, went to Grimsby the following spring and Sandra wanted us to go with him. I couldn't see how that could be a viable proposition. I was a police cadet, having taken that job after leaving school, and it meant just having lessons at the weekend. I didn't like the idea, either, of the small rink at Grimsby. Then the Nottingham rink manager arranged for Janet Sawbridge to take Mr Sayward's place and with her background she jumped at the chance, I think, of grooming possible successors, once Sandra had got the idea of Grimsby out of her system. Janet had only just turned professional.

The three of us were together for about a week before there was a final explosion and Sandra left. The chemistry wasn't right, never

(*below left*) Jayne, then a pair skater, with her first partner, Michael Hutchinson, at a Nottingham gala during her early teens; (*below right*) Chris's first title, British primary ice dance champion with Sandra Elson in 1972

really had been. A certain amount of disagreement is inevitable in these circumstances but it was getting to the point where Sandra and I would have a tiff and the whole training session would be lost in a fog of recrimination. I remained with Janet for a time on my own and got on really well with her, especially as she knew little of Nottingham and had few friends there. Then she had the brainwave, for which we can never thank her enough, of matching me with Jayne. 9

Jayne's reaction to the suggestion was one of excited enthusiasm. She recalls:

6I was delighted because I was getting to a loose end with figure skating. I had missed my chance in the junior championships and would have to get both silver and inter-gold tests to qualify in the seniors. It would be very difficult. I felt therefore that I'd come to the end of the road with figures, and ice dance seemed an inviting alternative. I can't say that I reasoned it out like that, but that was how my instincts led me. When I was little I'd always liked dancing anyway and I'd always taken to it quite easily. Even before that, when I was really tiny, I would watch the adults at dance intervals and when they'd finished I'd go on and try to copy their steps. A bit later on I'd done ice dancing for two or three years, but by the time of my teaming up with Chris I couldn't remember all the steps even of the dances I knew. Some, more recently introduced, were quite unknown to me. 9

For their early development we have to rely heavily on Jayne's memory because Chris cannot recall how the experiment that was to launch them to the stars began. One Wednesday night, after Chris had taken a lesson from Janet, she asked him and Jayne to stretch out their arms to see if they would be compatible. Had his arm been that much longer than Jayne's it would have been bent in the hold position while hers was straight and that would have produced an ugly line. Janet was apparently satisfied because, soon afterwards, a friend of hers asked Jayne if she would like to try her luck with Chris, an idea that had been vaguely in Jayne's mind from the time that Sandra had decamped. His blond good looks were a further incentive. Thus it was that the three of them assembled the following morning in May at six o'clock.

It was a sombre occasion, Jayne wondering if she would be out of her depth in a new discipline, Chris wondering if he had made a mistake and been driven into a corner by the absence of any obvious alternative. They were both painfully shy, a characteristic that remains with Jayne to some extent and that Chris has thrown off only with difficulty over the years. Nor was there any blinding revelation of what was to come from what happened on the ice. They did little more than skate around together, with an occasional three-turn thrown in. They did not dare dance together. The most important lesson from Janet Sawbridge, Jayne records, was that:

❝I had really to stretch my free leg to match Chris's and so eliminate as far as possible the physical disparity between us. I'm only 5ft 0½in, nearly ten inches shorter than Chris, and in the same position as Janet had been in her day. She was the same height as me and her second partner, Peter Dalby, was much taller even than Chris. The next evening was our first dance night. That was ghastly. Everybody was watching us so critically, it was like being put under a microscope. I hadn't danced for some time and even one of our friends, now an ex-friend as far as I'm concerned, said to Chris: 'I don't think she's going to be any good for you.' I fell during the blues and banged my head and elbow. I made as light of it as I could at the time, but nowadays I'd be moaning for hours. Perhaps we were too sensitive, but we had the feeling that people were thinking that Janet must have been off her rocker to think she could make something of us.❞

But from that tiny acorn of sporting endeavour a mighty oak was to grow, first under Janet Sawbridge's enthusiastic tutelage and later Betty Callaway's thoughtful guidance. After a couple of weeks Janet asked two judges, Michael and Kay Robinson, to look them over at one of their weekly visits to the Nottingham rink and offer an opinion. The Robinsons were non-committal. Chris:

❝They thought it was much too early to tell whether or not we would be likely to make a go of it. We were not surprised. We could not have looked too impressive, nor would we have expected to be in view of our lack of experience. I had done only one British championship and Jayne, of course, none at all. At least they did not throw in the black ball, which was a negative kind of encouragement.❞

By happy chance the Deans had arranged to move, before the partnership was formed, to within a few minutes' walk of the newsagents' shop that the Torvills had taken over three years previously. Now commuting between the two homes was reduced by about twenty minutes, an important consideration in view of the gallon of activity they were trying to squeeze into every pint pot of

Their first victory together, the Sheffield Trophy of 1976; second place was taken by Trevor Davies and Tandy Buxton, and third by Jeffrey Hayes and Julie Simpson (*Jack Holmes Photos*)

time. Jayne was also in full-time employment, in the offices of Norwich Union. At first they depended on their families to ferry them back and forth, but soon they learnt to drive and one by one the difficulties were being overcome. The closer proximity also meant that they saw more of each other off the ice and an even closer personal relationship developed.

Their first competition of any significance was a Bristol dance weekend in the autumn of 1975, four months after they had come together. They finished second to Nicky Slater and Kathryn Winter, the best result they could have hoped for since Slater and his partner won the bronze medal in the British championship that year. More to the point, Chris and Jayne beat couples of greater experience who would have been expected to finish above them. Janet Sawbridge was highly encouraged, for it was the spur they all needed to carry them through the hard slog of the winter of 1975-6.

They treasure a photograph taken at a competition in Sheffield, since—insignificant as it was—it brought them their first sentimental victory together. More important was their win in the Northern championship held, oddly enough, at Bristol in April 1976. Even if this is not quite what it seems, since skaters of senior standard would be aiming for the British title instead, it was a title— important to them and their self-respect at the time. The British title would have to wait for their acquisition of the inter-gold medal test.

By now skating was becoming a way of life. They so much enjoyed what they were doing and each other's company that they found they were seeking companionship elsewhere less and less often. A hectic social life would have been contrary to the routine into which they had fallen, a lesson every night from 7-7.30, followed by an hour and a half in the public session. There would be two hours on Thursday morning from 6.00-8.00 and a couple more on Monday morning. They skated on Sundays from 9.00 till noon.

Their new goal was the inter-gold, which they needed to compete in a British championship. When the day came Chris suffered a minor humiliation for he, the senior partner, unexpectedly failed the test while Jayne passed. Chris was out of luck because his test was taken first and the timing, for which both were responsible, was at fault, even after a reskate. Had Jayne been under the same scrutiny it would have been she who got the thumbs down. When they repeated the exercise, a rumba original dance, after rapid coaching by Janet Sawbridge, they got the timing right, but it was now Jayne who was under examination. Although Chris was unlucky to find himself in this position, he left the rink with lowered spirits and hurt pride. Further practice by both partners enabled him later to climb this hurdle and so claim a place in the British championship that year,

1976. The experience at least stood them in good stead in their first world championship in Ottawa the following season where the compulsory dances included the rumba which has a lilting echo in the exhibition rumba they developed later.

Then a new problem arose. Their respective salaries were modest but with few other claims on their purses they had been able to make ends meet with a little bit of help from their parents. But Chris learnt that in straitened times he could no longer rely on his father for support. It was now that Janet Sawbridge showed her integrity with an offer of free lessons—such was her enthusiasm for the young couple who had responded so conscientiously to her promptings. It is not uncommon in the ice-skating fraternity for teachers to help pupils in this way if they feel they have sufficient potential and dedication, and in the light of the rupture that was to come all too quickly it is only fair to record Janet Sawbridge's generosity.

So they were able to venture abroad for the first time together to Oberstdorf, later to become a home from home, and St Gervais, where summer competitions are held for those who are on the verge of the big break-through. Both had been abroad before with their former partners—Jayne had even taken part in the European pairs championships of 1972 at Gothenburg—but on all previous occasions they had been heavily chaperoned because of their youth. Now they were expected to take care of themselves.

For the National Skating Association (NSA) to have chosen them for Oberstdorf and St Gervais was a remarkable tribute to the advance they had made in only one year together. Certainly, both now express surprise that they were recognised so quickly. It was something of a vintage year in the Alpine resorts: besides Chris and Jayne the competitors included Robin Cousins, Olympic champion of 1980, and Scott Hamilton who, like them, was to win the world championship for the first time the next year. Getting to Oberstdorf in the first place was something of an adventure for the two wide-eyed innocents abroad and made heavy inroads into their shallow pockets. Jayne:

❦ The NSA paid half the cost, but that was refunded only on our return. We lived a spartan existence, but we were pushing back a frontier and ready to rough it for the sake of experience, as I've no doubt any eighteen-year-old would be prepared to. Chris was in fact only seventeen when we went, but he had a birthday while we were out there. In the absence of any more economical means of reaching Oberstdorf, we took a night flight to Zurich and slept rough at the airport from midnight until six o'clock before catching the first train to Oberstdorf, several hours away. At Oberstdorf the daily routine

With their first trainer, Janet Sawbridge, herself a former British champion (*Nottingham Evening Post Photos*)

of subsistence was to fill ourselves as much as possible with a breakfast of ham and eggs, raw ham and eggs really but we had to eat it or starve. We would buy one meal out, at the Nordsee, a fish and chip restaurant where a fishcake and a few chips would not run away with too many marks and pfennigs, and we would make do at other times with biscuits, brought from home, and coffee brewed surreptitiously in an hotel room.

It was a lifestyle far removed from the five-star treatment that is theirs by right today when sent abroad for competition or exhibitions, for which they are in huge demand. But they were young enough to put up with the hardship and enjoy the excitement and the freedom, since Janet Sawbridge had been unable to accompany them. In 1980, they came to know Oberstdorf intimately as a regular training ground. Their accommodation at the Internat Hotel, a part of the rink complex with facilities unmatched anywhere in the world, was, and still is, functional rather than luxurious; the meals were plain and monotonous enough for them to welcome an occasional spree in the town. In 1976 they were thrown together for the first time, discovered a mutual affection and developed a spirit of independence along the guidelines offered by Janet Sawbridge before they left home. They learnt how to fend for themselves, fight for themselves, plan their practices and prepare for competition without supervision—how to stand on their own two feet.

On the ice there was some disparity between the two, Chris being in his own words 'more dancified'. Jayne had regularly taken extra coaching from Janet Sawbridge, but it would take her a year or two to catch up her partner. At that point, approaching their first international examination, Chris was the more impressive of the two, especially to those who concentrated too little on what they were doing on the ice. Their results were highly encouraging. They were second at Oberstdorf to a Russian couple, Marina Zueva and Andrei Vitman, and beat into third place Carol Long and Philip Stowell who had been fifth in the British championship the previous winter.

There was a frustrating footnote the following March when Chris and Jayne sat at home watching Zueva and Vitman, not they thought appreciably their superiors, taking fifth place in the world championships in Helsinki. The Russians went home after Oberstdorf to be replaced by some useful Americans and Canadians, and left the way clear for St Gervais. Chris and Jayne seized the chance to record their first international win. Oberstdorf and St Gervais tend to throw up interesting results because international judges are often seeing skaters for the first time, without any preconceived ideas of their quality. So domestic results count for little. People at home began to take notice of this little-known Nottingham couple and consider their prospects. They had arrived.

Chris's principal memory of their first British championship in the autumn of 1976 was that they wore 'putrid green'. He can afford to take an amused view of their formative years and their lack of polish in so many directions. The time when they would be brought to recognise the value of attractive outfits, suitable hair styles and make-up for Jayne lay ahead. For the moment it was the skating that counted to them. They were fourth at Nottingham in their first British championship and they created a favourable impression with their performance of the Ravensburger waltz, introduced into the handbook by a former couple of Betty Callaway's, Erich and Angelika Buck. For these young pretenders to excel in a difficult new exercise, run at a faster tempo than today, was significant in a small way, and another tribute to Janet Sawbridge, herself a brilliant waltzer. Fourth place meant a nomination as reserves in the British team, though they would have to wait another year before they stepped into that higher arena.

Partnership under strain

They returned to Oberstdorf the following summer, 1977, and closed the gap created by Zueva and Vitman, but not before the partnership was strained almost to breaking point. Chris readily admits that they would have come to the end of the road in the summer of 1977 had it not been for the courage and determination of his partner. He explains:

❝ Until now my police cadet work had been confined to Nottingham. Now I had to take probationary training before I could become a police constable and that took me to Dishforth, two hours' drive away in Yorkshire, for ten weeks. It was a tough course, not only physically but mentally as well because it involved a lot of study. In the ordinary way I would have got home on the Friday and lolled away the weekend, recharging the batteries for another week of training. Instead, I had to throw myself into a hectic schedule of skating. I would arrive home on the Friday evening and have to leave immediately for the rink. Friday night's training was followed by more on Saturday morning and evening, and again on Sunday morning. Then it was time for me to leave for Dishforth, drained rather than recuperated.

What made it worse was that Jayne had been bored out of her mind during the week, not exactly stimulated by her humdrum work at Norwich Union, and only able to potter about at the rink on her own. I was fit to drop, she was raring to go. I regarded the police then as my career, of course, and it sometimes seemed pointless to flog myself at weekends and so jeopardise what I was doing through the week. I just don't know how I survived that period. What I do know is that if it hadn't been for Jayne's perseverance we would have been finished there and then. She's some girl, such a strong character. She may look small, even fragile—which in fact she is not—but she's all heart. More than once during those ten weeks I told her she ought to go and find another partner, but she would have nothing of it. Lucky me. ❞

They looked almost like being victims of their own virtues, for they had been chosen by the NSA again for Oberstdorf—St Gervais having already been conquered and offering no chance of their bettering themselves—and Chris was in no shape to make a special effort. Those ten weeks at Dishforth were followed by five marginally less harrowing weeks of local constabulary training at Epperstone before Chris became a policeman in earnest. Epperstone is near enough to Nottingham for Chris to commute for skating, though he had to live in. Jayne had to motor out to Epperstone about forty-five minutes away and bring Chris to Nottingham for a six o'clock start at the rink. He would then borrow her car to go back to Epperstone and reappear at the rink in the evening for further practice.

Contemporaries now testify to the steadfastness with which they faced those unsocial hours, leaving the rink as others arrived at a more civilised time, or when others were leaving for a conventional bedtime. Nottingham's charms must have been elusive when the rain beat down or the snow piled up at a time when most people were warmly tucked between the sheets. Time would release them from this bondage, but only after they had endured it conscientiously enough to have established their reputation. By now, Chris had become reconciled to keeping faith with Jayne. That was one worry off their minds.

The sacrifice Jayne made may be measured by the fact that even ordinary early-morning training, which they now resumed, was purgatory for her. She is one of the worst timekeepers in the world which must have made her later switch to 'flexi-time' with Norwich Union one of the jokes of the commercial world. On the other hand, Chris was punctual to a fault. To call for Jayne ten minutes too soon, even before the dawn came up, was to compound the misery of the early morning. She had to clonk downstairs from the family flat above her parents' newsagent shop to answer the call and this

Chris in his police days, third from right in back row.

added to her delay, particularly if, as was often the case, she was virtually sleepwalking and had forgotten to bring the key with her. With Chris full of beans and Jayne hardly able to open her eyes, it was a sure recipe for an acrimonious start to the day. She cheerfully confesses to a weakness here but claims, apparently with some justification, that she has never been late on the ice.

Oberstdorf in 1977 gave them their second international victory. It was to their advantage that they knew the ropes a little and this may have helped them to record the first of many successes over an ambitious American couple, Carol Fox and Richard Dalley. The Americans had won at St Gervais and were expected to add Oberstdorf to their laurels, but Chris and Jayne got the better of them in a taut struggle. The British championship followed at Nottingham and Chris and Jayne, assisted perhaps by a break-up of other partnerships, took the bronze medal and so claimed a place for the first time in the European and world championships which were to be held that winter in Strasbourg and Ottawa. Nicky Slater and Karen Barber, who were to be fellow members of the British team for several seasons to come, were fourth—they were skating together for the first time after rifts with their previous companions. It meant temporary relegation for Slater, who had been third in 1976 with his former partner.

As members of the British team Chris and Jayne came under wider scrutiny and two important new characters entered the story, two men whose talents lie in other directions as well as skating. They are Courtney Jones and Bobby Thompson: Jones is a former world ice dance champion, four times with two different partners; Thompson is a professional teacher whose principal charges at that time were Kay Barsdell and Kenny Foster, second in the British championship. Through Vera Pilsworth, a kind friend in many ways to Chris and Jayne, Jones and Thompson became involved in producing the outfits for the young Nottingham couple. Until then their dresses and suits were the product of a homespun cooperative involving a number of friends, Janet Sawbridge and the two skaters themselves. Only small changes could be made during that 1977–8 season but the full effect of the influence of Jones and Thompson would be clearly seen in the seasons that followed, and not merely in the matter of dress.

Now it was January 1978 and time to take off for their first European championships in Strasbourg. What did it mean to them? Jayne:

❻It was something that we'd only watched on television before. Now we were to be a part of it. At that time the stars were Irina

Bobby Thompson, one of a number of people who have provided valuable help to Chris and Jayne (*Ice & Roller Skate Magazine*)

Moiseyeva and Andrei Minenkov, a Russian couple with Bolshoi background. We'd watched them with total fascination, thought them fabulous. It was hard to believe that we were going now to share the same rink, the same dressing-rooms, the same audience, the same atmosphere. If we were never going to do anything else, the fact that we were going this once was a thrill. The worry now was that one of us might be taken ill or suffer some small injury that would stand in our way. There was, too, the matter of raising the money to enable Janet Sawbridge to come with us, and various fund-raising activities were undertaken.

But the Janet who came with us to Strasbourg was not the one we'd first known. She'd got married to a man outside the skating world and found it difficult to reconcile her work with changed domestic circumstances. Already her enthusiasm was declining. She'd always been mad-keen for us to do well and would have dragged herself to the rink if she'd been on the point of death. Now, the smallest excuse was enough to keep her away for a week. There was good reason. She was pregnant and had other things on her mind. It didn't help the situation that she was in a different hotel in

Strasbourg and we depended a good deal on Warren Maxwell and Janet Thompson, the British champions at the time, for general guidance. They introduced us to the people who mattered and were generally good companions. Warren, particularly, was always good for a laugh, without sacrificing anything in the way of dedication. He worked when he had to and enjoyed himself when he hadn't. No bad way to look at life. **9**

At Strasbourg they were terribly sporty and wore their tracksuits all the time, believing that to be the proper dress for the occasion; they spent much of their spare time jogging devotedly in the streets. These were practices they would abandon in a year or two, as do most experienced skaters. Then, it seemed the thing to do; later, they came to realise that if they were not fit before they arrived at a championship they could hardly improve matters within a week or so. Later, too, they were amused to see new arrivals going through the same ritual of introduction and in time turning to normal wear, their spare time being given over to sightseeing, shopping and general relaxation.

The European championships were a step on the road, but there was no hint of the triumphs to come. Ninth place enabled them to break through the psychological barrier of the 'top ten'. The significance of the top ten, though it did not apply to Chris and Jayne, is that the country concerned may enter two skaters, or couples or pairs, the following year instead of the minimum of one. They could hardly have hoped for more, given that they were bound to be preceded by three Russian and the top two British couples to start with. It was therefore no occasion for violent breastbeating, but a valuable experience all the same. Chris:

6 We felt so *small* in the dazzling company. When we got to see Moiseyeva and Minenkov on the ice for real, they were not only better than we had imagined, but they seemed so strong and powerful, and so big. Everybody seemed so much bigger than us, in fact, and if in many cases it was more imagined than real, in the case of Moiseyeva and Minenkov it was a fact. Minenkov must have been over six feet, which is unusually tall for a skater, and his wife (they were married during their skating career) was taller than average. She had to be, otherwise they would have looked unbalanced. As it was they looked fabulous, particularly Irina, beautiful and balletic, and I couldn't have conceived that anybody in the world, let alone us, would ever beat them. We were both quite bowled over by them. We'd heard Alan Weeks raving about them on the box so often. Now we really knew why. **9**

As is their earnest way, the young Britons looked and learnt in Strasbourg. Jayne:

❝All the top couples seemed so professional in their approach, so meticulous in their preparations, specially the Russians. I was fascinated, too, by the way the Hungarians Krisztina Regoeczy and Andras Sallay (then trained by Betty Callaway) approached the rinkside when they were due to skate. They walked down holding hands and I think he gave her a little kiss or something before they went on. It surprised me because everybody was supposed to be so aggressive and competitive. It was simply a matter of their doing their thing in their own way, because so far as I know they were not emotionally involved. All skaters, probably all sportsmen and women, have their little eccentricities and that was one of theirs. ❞

Krisztina Regoeczy and Andras Sallay, an Hungarian couple trained by Betty Callaway, who became close friends and mentors to Chris and Jayne (*All-Sport Photographic*)

Kris and Andy were to become firm friends and mentors of Chris and Jayne within a few months, but at that time they were virtually strangers and it seems odd for the British couple to look back and recall how noisily they rooted for Janet Thompson and Warren Maxwell, the Hungarians' closest rivals at Strasbourg. There was some friendly needle between the two couples because of their equality of performance in previous championships. It is a common practice for skaters to measure themselves and their progress against particular competitors and develop a personal rivalry. It is usually on a friendly level, though sometimes touched with envy and rancour.

Chris and Jayne have one harrowing memory of Strasbourg, skating the starlight waltz next to last among nineteen couples. It was the first of the compulsories and therefore their first exercise at this level. They were terrified at having to make their bow on ice that resembled the aftermath of a particularly boisterous public session. All those edges, after seventeen couples on hard ice with no resurfacing, Chris recalls, made them hold back for fear of a fall.

Resurfacing of ice is a thing they both feel strongly about, since it brings an unnecessary element of chance into the competition. The nervous tension for Jayne was such that she was exhausted after only about half of the first of three sequences. No doubt the poor training build-up also played a part. They had had such difficulty in reconciling the times of their jobs with ice availability that they had done much too little training for full physical condition. Compared with some others, Jayne insists, their hours of practice had been practically nil.

They returned from Strasbourg full of the thrill of it. They are unusually modest people but they were proud to be presented to the British public by way of television. It also had the side-effect of some good-natured ribbing of Chris among his colleagues in the police. Until then he had kept fairly quiet about his private passion, not because he is secretive by nature but simply because, like his partner, he is not the kind of person to gush or blow his own trumpet. One or two close friends were aware of his skating, but the main body of the force knew of it for the first time when they saw the championships on television. The winks and nudges flowed.

An unpleasant new shock awaited them. After Strasbourg they decided to go running every night to improve their fitness. It lasted only a week before Jayne suffered an injury. Chris:

❛ Jayne's right foot became inflamed and painful. I didn't take it all that seriously at first. It seemed to me that Jayne was not cut out for running, that was all. I was amazed, therefore, when she returned from hospital with her leg in plaster. I was so mad with her, may God forgive me, that I walked out of the room. That's all the sympathy she got from me. But this was two weeks before we were to leave for Canada, of all places, the other side of the world that we'd never seen and might never have another chance to see for all we then knew.

In fact, it looked worse than it was. The hospital had insisted that Jayne should not use her leg at all and to make sure she didn't they put it in plaster. We hid ourselves away for that week, never going near the rink, in case the word got around and the NSA decided to send somebody else in our place. When the plaster came off, Jayne still felt some pain and we could do only light training for a day or two. When we got going in earnest we seemed to have benefited from the lay-off, because our training went really well. We seemed much fresher and much faster. I suppose we'd had a long, hard season and we needed the break. It was a blessing in disguise. **9**

They saw less and less of Janet Sawbridge and can recall having only one lesson between Strasbourg and Ottawa, the day before they left for Canada. Her baby was due soon. If they were ill-prepared for Strasbourg, they did not expect the setback that happened in Ottawa. I met Jayne at the rinkside after their free dance on the last night and it was an embarrassing experience. They had skated well and my genuine offer of congratulations was met by an almost shell-shocked expression of dismay. 'But we've been beaten by the Handschmanns,' she replied, as if unable to believe the evidence of the computer that Susi Handschmann and her brother Peter, of Austria, had overtaken them. They had lain tenth after the first three compulsories but made such ground in the OSP (original set pattern dance) that they beat the second American couple, Stacey Smith and John Summers, lying a place above them. They were hopeful now of dislodging the Americans from ninth place after the free. They were shattered, as Jayne puts it, to find that they had been beaten into eleventh place in the free and fallen behind the Handschmanns in the overall positions. It had not even occurred to them to look over their shoulders to see what threat might lurk behind. Another setback was that Fox and Dalley, whom they had beaten at Oberstdorf, finished three places ahead of them.

Downcast as they were at the time, they can look back and see extenuating circumstances. They were not as fit as they should have been, because of their jobs and Jayne's injury; they had seen little or nothing of their teacher for a month or more—Janet Sawbridge was unable to go to Ottawa and they were placed under the care of another trainer, never a satisfactory alternative; and, to cap it all,

Chris had a heavy cold, easily acquired in a bitter Canadian winter where the river provided a solid natural skating rink many miles long for the hardy natives. Curiously, Chris's illness was at its worst on the day of the OSP when they achieved their best result of the competition. Chris had taken little or no medication, because of the fear of becoming ensnared in a drug test. The International Skating Union (ISU) is as strict as the International Olympic Committee in this area and, Chris says, 'you can safely take an aspirin and nothing else, that's about what it boils down to'. Shattered or not, they suffered no lasting damage to their morale, according to Jayne. 'We were so full of ideas, not precisely formalised plans, but a clear view of what we wanted to do and how we hoped to achieve it. We decided not to look back—but then we never do.' They returned home to discover they no longer had a teacher.

Janet Sawbridge (now Janet Salisbury) was in the maternity ward and Chris and Jayne went to visit her in hospital, Jayne clutching a present she had brought back from Ottawa. Janet told them she would be giving up teaching. A dramatic declaration like that ought to have been greeted with torment and tears, but Chris and Jayne felt overwhelming relief. Chris now sees it may have appeared selfish of them, but they knew at least the uncertainty was over. Jayne:

❢ Janet had made such a total and generous commitment to us for two years that it was hard to accept the change that occurred in the third, the intrusion of a third party. I surprised myself by the unemotional way I accepted Janet's withdrawal. I had expected to be upset, but in the event I felt my mind at rest. We wanted something concrete from Janet and now we'd got it. It was sad that the break had to come this way, leaving us all under a cloud, but I suppose it was inevitable from the moment of her marriage to a man who, whatever his other qualities, had no interest in her professional life. We shall, however, always be grateful to Janet Sawbridge. Without her intuition in bringing us together and her inspiration in giving us the will to overcome so many difficulties, we would almost certainly have individually ended up somewhere else, Chris probably sorting out traffic accidents and me the claims that followed. Alas, we have had no contact with her at all since the break, only a rather sour interview given to a local newspaper when we won our first European gold medal in 1981. ❢

In the absence of Janet Sawbridge we have to rely on others for an objective view of Chris and Jayne in those early international days. Joan Wallis, the British team manager in Ottawa, declared that 'the first time I saw Christopher Dean, and that was before Ottawa, I got

Chris and Jayne with their families, George and Betty Torvill (left) and Colin and Betty Dean (*All-Sport Photographic*)

the spark. He struck me as something quite special, because of his natural movement and poise and musical feel. Jayne was a fine technical skater whose personality did not show on the ice at that time.' Eileen Anderson, the manager in Strasbourg, recognised Jayne as 'the strong voice, very positive off the ice. She was always the one you would discuss things with. There came a point when you suddenly realised that somebody was standing nearby and you'd turn round to find Chris.' In time a balance would be struck, with Chris developing a strong personality off the ice and Jayne discovering how to project herself on it.

Betty Callaway

The dominant person in their lives was about to take the stage, not that anyone would easily see Betty Callaway in that light because she is as quiet and reserved as Chris and Jayne themselves. In their hour of need a number of names had occurred to them or been suggested. They included Hilary Green, a former world championship runner-up; Gladys Hogg, a revered figure at Queens, London; Joan Slater, trainer of the next British couple in line; and Bobby Thompson, also London-based. They all came to nothing mainly because Chris's police connection kept him in Nottingham.

Their first association with Betty Callaway was brought about by a dustbin in Ottawa. Jayne had carelessly left a dress draped over this unlikely clothes horse while waiting for an official bus at the rink. Betty came across it and recognised it as belonging to 'that new couple from England'. She had seen Chris and Jayne from a distance at Strasbourg and found them 'painfully shy. I didn't think they ever spoke to anybody.' She remembers saying to Krisztina Regoeczy and Andras Sallay, her Hungarian protégés at that time: 'I quite like the look of the third British couple. They're young and immature, but I think they've got something.' Their first words were exchanged in a lift at Ottawa; when Betty remarked on Chris's cold 'he only just about managed to answer me'.

Shortly after returning home the strands came together. Now at a loose end, Chris and Jayne sought help from Roy Sanders, manager of the Nottingham rink, and the upshot was a call to the Beaconsfield home of Betty Callaway. Would she be interested in throwing a lifeline to a deserving young couple in distress? Believing herself to be free of all other commitments—wrongly as it turned out—Betty discussed the proposition with her husband Bill Fittall, a retired British Airways captain (she keeps the professional name of her first marriage) and went up the following week to meet Chris and Jayne. It was the start of an unimaginably successful partnership, even supplanting all the popular group sports in winning the award of Team of the Year by the British Sports Writers' Association for the first time in 1981 in the wake of their first world title.

Unusually for a teacher, Betty Callaway had no career as an amateur skater. Within four months of attending Queens with a convent school party for the first time, she had walked out of school at the age of sixteen and ventured north for the brashness and bright lights of Blackpool. 'I couldn't skate,' she cheerfully confesses, 'but I could do a waltz jump, three-turns and spirals, and that was enough for the chorus of a show.' It was not quite enough, but she had an equally essential attribute. We have it on the authority of her first husband Roy, one of the principals in the show, that Betty Roberts as she was then was a stunningly pretty girl, with a beautiful face, striking figure and the kind of cool air of good breeding that was likely to sway any doubts when the time came for interviews. To this day she carries her years and her looks well.

Her parents were angry with her—'specially as they had paid the term's school fees in advance!'—but she had the bug and there was nothing they could do to dissuade her. Perhaps such a break would cause even more tears these days when the world of ice skating is open to anyone who has the talent, dedication, and a little bit of help from family, friends and authorities. At that time skaters tended to come from the better-off homes, so the cultural shock of Blackpool's tinsel and feathers was something of a shared experience. Roedean accents are not all that common these days, nor is there any reason why they should be. Betty's parents relented somewhat when she returned home for the winter clearly none the worse for wear and took lessons from Gladys Hogg at Queens. She went back to Blackpool the following summer 'with a slightly better part' since she now stepped out of the chorus for one number with Roy, who had fallen in love with Betty.

Two more summers followed at Blackpool. The first in 1948 was highlighted by her marriage to Roy and the second by a disaster at the Blackpool rink. As they were leaving the rink one night during the summer of 1949, Betty tilted her nose in the air, sniffed suspiciously and asked Roy: 'Can you smell burning?' He could not and off they went to their digs. The next morning their landlady brought them up a newspaper announcing that the rink had burnt down during the night.

During the previous two winters they had taken jobs at the old Purley rink. Now they decided that they would like to teach full-time and secured positions at Richmond. They were quite well paid—although the changing value of money may be gathered from Betty's declaration at the time that 'if we can earn £20 a week between us we're made'. Within six months they were so made. In order to equip themselves better they took the various medal tests, in Roy's case only the gold which he passed with Gladys Hogg. Betty had more leeway to make up, though the three-turns and waltz jumps had long since ceased to hold any terrors for her. She took her gold medal test in 1953, two years after Roy.

Betty taught at Richmond for nineteen years before being

Betty Callaway in her days as a professional skater, with her first husband, Roy (right); they are accompanied by Joan Tomlinson and Charles Woodfield, and wear their costumes from the Blackpool ice show in a gala at Purley in 1950 (*Ice & Roller Skate Magazine*)

appointed national trainer in West Germany in 1971. During those years at Richmond she had a number of distinguished pupils, including Prince Charles, Princess Anne and John (later Sir John) Mills. Princess Anne was with her for three winters, when she mastered the waltz, two-step and fox-trot, and when she went off to Benenden Betty was among the group of specialist teachers who were invited to a cocktail party given by the Queen at Buckingham Palace. Another royal pupil was Viscount Linley, son of Princess Margaret and Lord Snowdon.

Teaching together, the Callaways produced one couple who won a world championship bronze medal in 1964, Yvonne Suddick and Roger Kennerson. That was the summit of their joint success at home, but the spread of their activities to the other side of the channel brought greater distinction. First Betty's German couple, Erich and Angelika Buck, won the European championship and were second in the world in 1972, and later Krisztina Regoeczy and Andras Sallay halted the Russian domination of the world championships in 1980, before handing over to Chris and Jayne. Betty had inherited the Hungarian couple from Roy who had been unable to resist a lucrative offer from Italy in 1975. Matilde Ciccia, a joyfully uninhibited exhibitionist, and Lamberto Cesarani made Roy the offer on the condition that he would cease to teach the Hungarians, the Italians' principal rivals at the time.

A week or two's reconnaissance in Milan was necessary before the deal could be completed and, since Roy was otherwise engaged,

Betty went on his behalf to see the lie of the land. She liked what she saw, the money was too good to refuse and Roy suggested to Betty that she should take over the Hungarians. That quick trip to Milan had reawakened Betty's enthusiasm and she readily agreed. The rest is future perfect. Not only did Regoeczy and Sallay rise to the top but Betty was on hand when Chris and Jayne were looking for someone to replace Janet Sawbridge.

Roy believes, surprisingly, that Betty is an outstanding trainer because she had no natural talent herself. She had to acquire the skill, partly by the cut-and-thrust of what happened on the ice, but also because her inner wisdom forced her to work things out for herself. She wanted to know why as well as how. Naturally talented skaters never know the agony of experiment or the requirement of intelligent analysis, so they are less able to impart the knowledge to pupils. It is a subtle twist on the cynical maxim that 'those who can, do; those who can't, teach'. It follows that Betty is strong in the compulsories, where the straitjacket of ISU instruction imposes severe disciplines. For free dancing she is more of a consultant, judging whether or not this or that creation will be effective.

Her calm temperament is a lifeline in periods of stress. 'Some trainers,' Roy believes, 'are so strung up at the time of competition that they manufacture tension themselves. Betty is so cool, so tactful, that no skaters, speaking in present terms, could be better prepared for competition than Chris and Jayne.' Roy believes that Chris and Jayne would have made it without Betty, 'but she has been a powerful influence for good for them, not only on the ice but in gradually wearing away their understandably provincial image and replacing it with a sophisticated polish.' The Callaways' marriage lasted 27 years, but they have remained such firm friends that the parting has left no scar. They kept the separation and divorce quiet in order to spare Roy's mother unnecessary distress. When Betty later married Bill Fittall, Roy became his friend. They are all civilised people.

At that first meeting with Chris and Jayne at Nottingham in 1978, Betty was not so much concerned about their ability as skaters as with other characteristics:

❢ With me, I'd got to like them as people first and foremost. If you only take one couple [she was unaware at that point that Regoeczy and Sallay would return] everything's wrapped up in them. You spend so much time with them that you must be compatible. You've got to like them and they've got to like you. You become a lot more personally involved. Well, I found them easy to work with on the ice, as technicians, and when later we talked things over in the

41

Nottingham rink cafeteria I saw them to be thoroughly nice, down-to-earth people, genuine and keen.

Yes, we decided we'd give it a try. I'd never had a British couple of my own before and that was an added spur. We came to a financial understanding which didn't weigh too heavily on them. I didn't want to make money out of them, but of course I didn't want it to cost me money. They were being helped by grants at various times from the NSA, the Nottinghamshire County Council and the Sports Aid Foundation. The normal routine would be for me to go up to Nottingham at weekends and leave them to work on set exercises during the week on their own. **9**

Betty then discovered that the retirement of Regoeczy and Sallay had been a misunderstanding, caused by the misreading of a letter from Mrs Regoeczy, although she speaks excellent English. 'Had she known,' Jayne says, 'she would not have committed herself to us, but she had now done so and is not the kind of person to let people down. The Hungarians would be her number one priority but she would still meet her responsibility to us.' What could have proved an embarrassment was turned to advantage by the rapport that quickly developed between the two couples.

That first summer Regoeczy and Sallay commuted to Nottingham with Betty at weekends, but the following summer they spent the whole time in the city. Before long Chris and Jayne saw the advantage of having them around. During the week they were thrown together with Betty back home in Beaconsfield, and Kris and Andy, as well as becoming firm friends off the ice, took a lively interest in Betty's new charges. There were other advantages; because Kris and Andy were sophisticated people, their style and polish began to rub off on Chris and Jayne. Without being affected, they began to find some self-confidence in other people's company.

It was not entirely one-way traffic. Any competitor gets an added stimulus in the company of others and in some respects Chris and Jayne could teach the Hungarians a thing or two about some of the compulsory dances even at that early stage. Betty would sometimes bring in the British couple as an example for the Hungarians to follow. Chris sums up his first impression of Betty as follows:

6 She taught me to think for myself when things were going wrong, whereas before I was always told 'Don't do this, do that', not a

Betty Callaway and her two prize charges relaxing outside their training head-quarters at Oberstdorf before the 1983 world championships (*All-Sport Photographic*)

42

question of 'Don't do this because..' and '...will happen if you don't to it like this'. She broke everything down and would ask 'Why do you think it's happening?' That's helped us because now we can work out when and where we may be going wrong and change it ourselves. For the free dance she gave us some general guidance but she didn't do any steps. She told us she thought our programme for Strasbourg and Ottawa had been a bit 'pair-skatey', with lots of side-by-side holds and straightforward runs to get speed. She made us aware of the holds we got into when we were making up a new programme, making sure we had a real dance movement. Ottawa aberrations were squashed. This does not imply any criticism of Janet Sawbridge. It was simply a phase we had to go through. It wasn't wrong for that time but had we done it again the following year it would have been wrong. Without being 'pair-skatey' to begin with we might have been less adventurous after that. **9**

The pattern soon developed. Betty was a compulsory dance specialist and she would drill them in the precise requirements set down by the ISU. So far as free dance and OSP were concerned, she believes in allowing skaters to express their own personalities. Since Chris and Jayne, particularly Chris, were full of ideas, the formula worked like a charm. The skaters would invent; the teacher would approve or not as the case might be. Betty was scarcely more demonstrative on the ice than off it, never one to lose her temper or create a scene. Yet she had her own quiet way of letting Chris and Jayne know when her patience was wearing thin. That would usually happen when there was a disagreement between Chris and Jayne rather than between them and her.

Chris can be a firebrand on the ice when things just will not fall into place, a cross every couple has to bear with something as creative as ice skating. But when he is on the verge of blowing his top Betty steps in.:

6 I take him to one side and say: 'Look, Chris, enough.' I never resent his behaving like that, or occasionally Jayne, because if there isn't some sort of temperament there they would never be the artists they are. I never shout on the ice. As soon as I've said my piece, we're back to normal, and never, but never, do they carry a disagreement off the ice with them. All this I allow at normal practice, but I have a strict rule about championships. They can have their occasional spit at home, perhaps they have to if they are to get anywhere, but once we get to the championships there must be no arguments on the ice. In the hotel room, if necessary, but never when the judges, the public and the press might be around. I admire tremendously the way Jayne

44

can take it without letting it carry over when they leave the ice. That shows some strength of character, but then she is a girl of character, of two characters in fact. On the one hand she can be a little girl, asking for an ice cream in a tiny child-like voice; on the other there's great determination and resilience. She's a super girl, with the right sort of principles. **'**

Chris's police duties seemed strangely at odds with the romantic nature of his sport. By now he was doing shift work with central division:

'I was on the beat, doing anything and everything that you can imagine a policeman doing, besides escorting old ladies across the road and rescuing cats from trees. We had a lot of shoplifters in the daytime, when somebody would catch some poor, wretched woman—it was usually women—in the act of nicking a packet of tea or a bar of chocolate. There were a lot of public order offences, drunkenness and things like that. At weekends we ran into a lot of offences against the person, ABH and GBH.

Fortunately, we did not get too involved with football crowds, because we were off the division where the games were played and our concern was to shepherd them in and out of the town. But if they arrived early they would all come straight into the city, get a drink or two inside them before the match and end up in the middle fighting. Sometimes I got involved in the struggle and took a few knocks but nothing serious enough to put me off duty. With shifts from 8am–4pm, 2pm–10pm or 5pm–1am and Jayne still doing basic 9am–5pm we had problems finding time to train. Sometimes Jayne would wangle a morning off by combining certain break periods, but at other times we could not find the time to train at all. **'**

Changing uniform and character, Chris managed somehow to prepare with Jayne to win their first competition under Betty Callaway's direction, the John Davis Trophy—a formality since they were the only British team members in the competition. Maxwell and Thompson, the British champions, were above the battle and Barsdell and Foster had retired, so Chris and Jayne were ranked second in Britain. Nevertheless they took great pride when they saw the names already inscribed on the trophy, such as Lawrence Demmy, Courtney Jones and Bernard Ford, together with their various partners. Anything that put them in that company had to be appreciated.

In those early days Betty saw Jayne as the stronger skater, 'more sure-footed, cleaner and more positive in the turns'. That summer

Betty demonstrates a technical point for Jayne's benefit at Oberstdorf (*All-Sport Photographic*)

(1978) they sought guidance from Gideon Avrahami, a Ballet Rambert teacher at Loughborough with ice experience. In itself, it was not perhaps earth-shattering but it pointed to a restless desire to leave no stone unturned in their search for improvement. Avrahami was the first of several men who made them aware of the body and arms, of the need to fit them into the whole picture. In November 1978 they became British champions. Maxwell and Thompson were unable to defend because of injury, but it might be unfair to assume that Chris and Jayne won by default. They had improved markedly in that first summer with Betty Callaway and the performance of Maxwell and Thompson at the Rotary Watches International (now the St Ivel) at Richmond a month or so earlier had not been all that impressive. Maxwell fell during the free and they hung on by the strength of their compulsories.

Chris and Jayne were regarded as worthy winners by many people, even milking their first 6.0 out of one judge, Mollie Phillips. There was a tendency at the time not to take this too seriously, for Miss Phillips is given to excessive generosity in moments of exhilaration. With hindsight, it looks positively prophetic. Nor should we dismiss the 5.8 and 5.9 from Courtney Jones, a man who has never given a six in his life.

In January 1979 the new British champions made the first of several trips to Budapest with Betty, Kris and Andy, and Chris was given much encouragement by a meeting with Zoltan Nagy, a celebrated ballet dancer who helped the Hungarian couple with their choreography. From him Chris learnt that a man could show grace and emotion without it being regarded as effeminate. Nagy took an instant liking to Chris, whom he dubbed the Blond Prince. According to Betty Callaway, there was an immediate sharpening of Chris's personality.

The European and world championships at the start of 1979 carried no great significance for Chris and Jayne. They moved up to sixth in Europe in the absence of Maxwell and Thompson, and eighth in the world with Maxwell and Thompson back on the ice. The Handschmanns were duly mastered at Zagreb, but bounced back momentarily—to no great surprise—in their native city of Vienna to push Chris and Jayne back to eighth. On the other hand Smith and Summers, the American champions, and Fox and Dalley were overtaken. The Austrians, together with Smith and Summers, would soon disappear from the scene, but Fox and Dalley would continue to make unsuccessful attempts to close the gap between them and the British couple. By now Chris and Jayne were touching 5.5 out of a maximum mark of 6.0 for their free dance.

They had settled into a routine at competition that has become a ritual. It seemed to be serving them well and, without being superstitious, they did not fancy tempting providence by ringing the changes. They will always lace up the left boot first, probably a natural inclination for right-handers but Jayne is left-handed, as anyone could guess from the way she attacks a piece of meat on her plate with the knife and fork held conventionally but clumsily in the 'correct' hands. Chris always wears the same pair of St Michael pants, of Cambridge blue.

The guiding principle in matters like this is that you keep to any winning combination. Sportsmen and women in other fields act similarly. The brand new cricket bat that gives a catch is apt to be regarded with suspicion; the putter that fails to hole out as often as its golfing owner thinks reasonable is consigned to the attic to gather rust for the rest of its days; the preliminary tap of the toe that first helped to launch a rugby penalty goal is regarded thereafter as indispensable to the success of the operation. One member of a famous British badminton women's doubles team used to tap her partner's bottom at crucial moments.

So Chris now has to step on to the ice with his left foot. Once he left the ice and returned after inadvertently taking off with the right foot. Jayne is unaware of any preference. The skate guards have to be laid on the floor by the rink with precision. Chris collects his partner's guards (which pleases her because they are apt to make the hands dirty) and places them down on the right-hand side of his, facing the rink. At Hartford in 1981 when they won the world championship for the first time, the guards were swept aside by a careless hand and had to be restored to their proper position by Betty Callaway without the skaters' knowledge. Back in the dressing-room Jayne's fortunes are always presided over by her three little 'paddy bears', clad in oilskins and wellies, tucked away in her skate bag. The bag itself is resplendent with ribbons that remain from the bouquets accompanying her gold medals in Europe and the world.

As a final protection against evil spirits Jayne wears gold skate earrings. According to Chris, they are 'dead men's teeth', since they were given to Jayne by the father of her former pairs partner, Michael Hutchinson, a dental technician. They are permanent accessories since the evening at Streatham when Jayne forgot to put them on after washing her hair and fell over during their exhibition. 'I've never been without them,' says this convinced opponent of superstition. Except for a sauna, she will never remove the necklace bearing a gold medal she bought in Ottawa to commemorate her first world championships.

Before they take the ice Betty Callaway will pat them on the back and say 'skate well'; never 'good luck'. The days when she used to arm herself also with a needle and thread to repair split seams in Chris's trousers are long gone. No need for her, as Jayne puts it, 'to freak out' with alarm as a gap appears. Betty used to carry a bracelet in her pocket bearing gold coins of various countries, a carry-over from her Regoeczy–Sallay days. 'It doesn't work for us,' Chris says. It seemed to bring them bad luck in the matter of draws for skating order and she was politely advised by Chris 'not to bother with that in future'.

Zagreb and Vienna were significant for Moiseyeva and Minenkov. They had been beaten in the world championships the previous year by their compatriots, Natalya Linichuk and Gennadi Karponosov. A second defeat by the same couple at Zagreb and being dislodged from second place in the world by Regoeczy and Sallay confirmed that their dazzling day was drawing to a close. The couple whom Chris and Jayne had felt to be safe from defeat for all time were on the way down in one short year. 'It was sad in a way,' Jayne says, 'because they had done so much for ice dance and, as we were to realise later, were smashing people.' That season also marked the end of Maxwell and Thompson. From second in Tokyo in 1977, they had dropped to fourth in Ottawa and fifth in Vienna. Thenceforth Chris and Jayne were number one in Britain.

Irina Moiseyeva and Andrei Minenkov, unbeatable in the view of Chris and Jayne at Strasbourg in 1978, but ranked only third the following year (*Colorsport*)

Growing up

Jayne began to blossom in the summer of 1979, partly as the result of advice given by Lawrence Demmy, a former world champion for Britain and the chairman of the ice dance committee of the ISU. Demmy was consulted by Betty Callaway and he felt that the most important step forward they could make was to project Jayne more positively. Her hairstyle was too tomboyish, he thought, she hardly wore any make-up, even under the powerful rink lights, and her dresses made little impact. Demmy says:

❛ Jayne has a nice face but she wasn't making the best of it. She seemed inhibited and unaware of the wonderful ability that was waiting to be brought out. Later we saw the end result. She has now got—and it's hard to believe after that uncertain start—tremendous sex appeal. And because she began to look good, she began to feel good and because of that her personality grew. She's always had a great technical ability, a very strong skater, but she didn't know what to do with it. It's one thing being able to skate on deep edges, another thing to be able to express the character of the music. This is what ice dancing is all about. They developed—and I say it with due consideration—into the best ice-dance couple the world has ever seen. In their different ways Ford and Towler, world champions from 1966 to 1969, followed by Pakhomova and Gorschkov (1970–4 and 1976) and then Moiseyeva and Minenkov (1975 and 1977), made a lasting mark on the sport, but if you could resurrect their best performances and put them beside those that Chris and Jayne produce now you can have no doubt which are superior. ❜

They broke fresh ground that summer with a trip to Hérisau, near Lake Constance in Switzerland. A teacher there had bought ice time while the rink was closed for the summer and had invited Betty to go there to teach. Kris and Andy were automatically invited, all expenses paid, but Betty pointed out that she now had a second couple under her wing. Yes, she could bring them along, too; they would also be able to set a good example for the Swiss. It was a boon, giving them two weeks' concentrated skating with plenty of ice time. Zoltan Nagy went too and that enabled them to do more work with him. It was another beneficial spin-off from the international connections that Betty Callaway had built up.

Chris and Jayne made significant strides during the 1979–80

season. In their first Rotary Watches competition they beat Kris and Andy in the free dance. The Hungarians had been second in the world championship in Vienna and they would be the next world champions in Dortmund the following March. 'The children', as Betty Callaway used to call Chris and Jayne in the presence of Kris and Andy, were growing up fast.

The next couple to receive a fright from 'the children' were Moiseyeva and Minenkov, who beat them only by three judges to two in the NHK Trophy competition in Tokyo in November. This was all the more praiseworthy because the Tokyo competition is confined to OSP and free dance, thereby depriving Chris and Jayne of the advantage they might expect to gain in the compulsory dances, the weakness of all Russian couples. Given the awe which they had once felt for Moiseyeva and Minenkov, it amounted to upstart impertinence. They also struck a blow for the Callaway stable and gladdened their trainer's heart by undermining the Russians' position *vis-à-vis* Regoeczy and Sallay with the European, world and Olympic competitions to come.

The British championship had been a formality since, with the retirement of Maxwell and Thompson, there were no serious challengers to the supremacy of Chris and Jayne. They were remembered more now for the quality of their skating than the result they achieved or the colour of the outfits they wore. They were not the couple in green, or red, or whatever any more, but the couple who brought jazz to free dance with an interpretation of Glen Miller's 'In the Mood' and Benny Goodman's 'Sing, Sing, Sing'.

There was originality of mind as well as skill of performance. They had been encouraged to go to the other extreme by the criticisms of pair-skating elements the year before. Nobody could see any suspicion of pair skating in the jive and swing of their free dance this time. Indeed, they received another 6.0 from Mollie Phillips. That had happened the year before, but their two 5.9s from Pamela Davis in the OSP were like getting blood out of a stone. They were making this impressive headway in spite of their difficulties with their jobs. Skating was becoming a dominant interest and Chris's dedication to the police force was taking a battering:

‘It was getting to the stage whereby I feared having to take somebody into custody at, say, 9 o'clock on the 2–10pm shift. Although I never walked away from an incident, I didn't much relish the idea. It meant that I might take custody of a prisoner either until the inquiries were finished or he was bailed to a court or kept in custody overnight. In one week alone I had to make three arrests which caused cancellation of training. There's a lot of paperwork, a lot of

Line-up at the British championship at Nottingham in 1979; from left Mark Reed, Karen Roughton, John Philpott, Carol Long, David Buckingham, Daphne Cronhelm, Nicky Slater, Karen Barber, Chris, Jayne, David Dagnell and Denise Best (*Nottingham Evening Post Photos*)

interviewing, and you've still got a prisoner next morning if he hasn't been bailed. You've got to deal with it then. I was under pressure because I was still in my probationary period. **,**

New doors were opening to them, as British champions, even the door of Number 10 Downing Street, where they attended a reception given for the departing cricket team to Australia. It was, of course, an exciting experience. Chris was astonished at the size of the place. 'Going through that front door was like entering Doctor Who's Tardis. It seemed to go on for ever. And all those photographs on the staircase! Mrs Thatcher made everyone feel at ease, whizzing around dispensing drinks and convivial small talk. I don't know how much homework she'd done, but as soon as we gave our names she remembered me as the policeman.'

Jayne went to the bathroom and 'that was nice, really nice. Lots of gold taps and things, gold door handles. Think of the people who must have used it! The Prime Minister was charming, the obvious star of the whole show, with everybody looking in her direction, in spite of how famous they were in their own fields, superstars like Ian Botham, Sebastian Coe, Willie Carson. It was our party, she said, not hers. And yet, I'm afraid, it became a bit of a bore. We were the only skaters, because Robin Cousins and Karena Richardson, the solo champions, were in the States and our pairs champions were too young for that sort of show. We felt rather lost and were quite happy to slip away for dinner with John Hennessy in a quaint

French restaurant near the Young Vic.'

They might by now have had stars in their eyes, having come so far so quickly. They had scared both the Hungarians and the second Russians and that left the world champions, Linichuk and Karponosov, as their prime target—with the possible exception of a couple from Czechoslovakia. But, they say, they still had no particular thought of winning the world title. They were surprised how quickly they put behind them the encouraging signs raised by Richmond and Tokyo. They are such realists that they still saw themselves as underdogs, 'with the nice feeling,' Jayne records, 'of pushing the others around a bit.' There's a certain ambivalence about Jayne's impression that 'it'd be nice to be up there with them, but at the time you realise it's more fun to be underneath, snapping away at their heels'. In time they would come to know the isolation and pressure of being at the top, while others had the fun.

At the European championships of 1980 at Gothenburg, Chris and Jayne beat Liliana Rehakova and Stanislav Drastich of Czechoslovakia for the first time. It was another rung up the ladder, to be surprisingly reversed a few weeks later in the Olympics at Lake Placid. At Gothenburg Chris was taken ill again with a bad stomach, probably a psychosomatic condition since he is rarely less than robustly healthy at times other than competition weeks. He has a touch of hypochondria, fearing illness or injury at the time of an important engagement and can be abrupt with people who, he feels, are careless about the possibility of spreading infection. A sneeze in a lift is apt to throw him into a tizzy.

At Gothenburg Chris lived on boiled rice and black tea for four days, so that 'by the time the competition started he was really skinny' according to his partner. Nevertheless, their marks showed a significant jump with nothing below 5.1 in the compulsories for the first time. Compulsories are always harshly marked compared with the OSP and free dance. They climbed to 5.7 in eleven instances for the free dance, for which Chris had recovered. They skated particularly well in the OSP fox-trot, a new tempo which bewildered many competitors that year. They found a lovely German recording of 'On a Little Street in Singapore' and let it flow. Until now their free dance had been less strong than their compulsories, but now they were achieving a balance. 'The children' were coming of age.

They have mixed views of their first Olympics at Lake Placid in February 1980. It was a big thrill but not an undiluted pleasure from the moment they climbed into a warm aircraft for Montreal clad as though for the North Pole, from fur-hatted heads to moon-booted feet, with a variety of shirts, sweaters and anoraks in between. It was the kind of protection they would need for a New York State winter,

but not designed for air travel. Even the Lake Placid organising committee, with their great gift for making a mess of things, could not entirely destroy their pride in representing their country, especially on this first occasion. It is a privilege to be a part of the Olympic movement, but in their blacker moments some of the athletes and the press would have wished themselves somewhere other than Lake Placid. A shiver still racks Jayne when she recalls the misery of the opening ceremony:

❛Heaven knows why, but we had to get started hours and hours before the business was to begin. First we were shoe-horned into buses and sat there in full uniform and acute, overheated discomfort for two hours before moving off. When the whistle eventually blew, we formed part of a funereal procession that seemed to take ages to get us to the arena for the opening ceremony. Another hour in the buses, which by now had been transformed into mobile saunas, and then we were decanted for the assembly before marching into the stadium. There we now stood for another hour in temperatures of minus I don't know what. My fingers began to ache with what seemed like frostbite, so much so that I was in tears. Eventually we were poured back into the buses for the return journey and the heat brought new pain to my hands.

I had been so excited about the Games eventually opening—we had arrived early for physical acclimatisation but much too early to retain a competitive edge—that I was deeply depressed in the end. I still wonder how many competitors were struck down by the experience, those hours of stifling heat in the buses, interspersed by a long period of Siberian chill. No wonder one of the leading characters on the organising committee, incredibly, had advised the public to stay away—and this in a country that prided itself in getting things done, making things happen. ❜

If it had not been for Betty Callaway's Hungarian connection, Chris and Jayne would have spent even longer waiting around for transport from the village (which has since been used as a prison) to the rink and back. The Hungarian party was so small that there was usually room for 'the children' too. On the ice they had mixed fortunes, overtaking another couple who had previously beaten them, Lorna Wighton and John Dowding of Canada, but allowing Rehakova and Drastich to slip in front of them again. The Czechoslovaks, surprisingly, had dredged up a song from the

The way they were—in 1979—Jayne unshorn, Chris uncoifed, both uninhibited as young challengers thrusting their way to the top (*All-Sport Photographic*)

Victorian music hall to finish off their free dance—'Won't You Come Home, Bill Bailey'—and had made a roaring success of it. It seemed to evoke an answering echo in Prague, because Mrs Drastich asked if she could have her husband back with the result that the charming Liliana Rehakova was deserted by her partner after Lake Placid. So one possible obstacle to the growing stature of the Nottingham couple was removed.

There was a solid array of 5.7s for the free dance and an average of 5.62. This compares with an average of 5.31 during the previous world championship, a spectacular improvement in one year. Fifth place or no, it was another cause for encouragement and might have received greater attention had it not been for the fact that all British attention in Lake Placid was focused on Robin Cousins and his gold medal. According to Eileen Anderson, the team leader in Lake Placid, 'many people felt that Chris and Jayne should have got on the podium'. It seemed an optimistic judgement at the time, implying the downfall of not only the Czechoslovaks but also Moiseyeva and Minenkov, but then we were not to know that everyone would be surrendering to Torvill and Dean within a year.

But their Olympic memories tend to linger on other activities, a gruelling attempt, for instance, at one of the cross-country courses, causing Jayne to remark: 'When I tell my grandchildren that I went round the Olympic course ...', apparently unaware of the fact that she will have other, more compelling, tales to tell.

Chris and Jayne learnt to distinguish between the different teams by their accents. The cross-country team, Jayne says, 'were all privates and spoke like what we do' whereas the bob boys would bid you 'Oh, hello' (and here she plays the part to perfection) in a languid public-school drawl. They recognised the disadvantage of being ice dancers (or pair skaters) because of the Olympic segregation of the sexes. Women may visit the men's quarters but never may the men claim equal rights, so that a good deal of forethought and planning were necessary to avoid tedious treks across the sexual divide, or a shorter trudge through deep snow. They became obsessively aware of the need for the 'stupid little tag round our necks' to avoid falling foul of the inflexible security system. Jayne 'couldn't get over the plastic cutlery, because I have enough trouble with a knife and fork at the best of times'.

Back home again, Jayne found her employers less generous than Chris's in giving her time off. When she returned to the office on the

Performing the starlight waltz at the European championships at Gothenburg, 1980
(*Colorsport*)

day after touching down at Heathrow airport, she found she spent half of the time in conversation with her friends, all eager to hear about the Olympics, and the other half nodding off at her desk. Chris, on the other hand, was on duty in Nottingham only for a couple of days in the two weeks between the Olympics and the world championships at Dortmund. He was now 'on the square', rotating with two other police constables in keeping the peace in the city centre and was one of the two central characters in an episode one summer Sunday that might have been lifted intact from the Keystone Kops. At such a time of year Nottingham is a typical British city, with the Salvation Army band playing in the middle of the square, family parties at one end and drunks and down-and-outs at the other. Into this motley gathering strode one Winston. Chris takes up the story:

❝It was a hot day and I took no great notice at first when he took his shirt off. Then he kicked his shoes off, so I watched him a bit more carefully and when he started going towards his trousers I felt I'd better close in. I threaded my way through the families, the band and the 'toe-rags', by this time studying Winston with growing uneasiness. There must have been a hundred people on the square at the time. Then he stripped off completely and started jumping up and down and parading about. He'd just popped his cork. He'd been a perfectly sane man until this time but the hot weather apparently got to him, for all his West Indian origin, and he went bananas. When I reached him I ordered him to put his clothes on in as authoritative a voice as I could muster, but of course he took no notice.

It's impossible to dress a man who doesn't want to be dressed, so I put him on the floor on his front and called for a van over the walkie-talkie. The inspector came down and we put him in the back of the van. By this time I'd had ten minutes on the square with everybody howling and laughing, jeering and cheering, with the Salvation Army beating a hasty retreat. We drove off and were moving down a four-lane, one-way street when Winston discovered that we'd omitted to lock the van and made a bolt for it as we slowed up at some traffic lights. We then had to chase him, still starkers, through the lines of heavy traffic and there was another struggle before we overpowered him, a hard, stocky man. A week later, to go to the other emotional extreme, I heard that he'd died after being taken to a mental hospital. ❞

During the weeks between the Olympics and the world championships they had tried a different training routine. Until then, they had skated from 10.30 on most nights; now they got up at about 3.00am

Jayne welcomed back by her Norwich Union colleagues after the 1980 Olympics at Lake Placid (*Nottingham Evening Post Photos*)

in the morning and skated from 4.00–6.00am, whereupon Chris resurfaced the ice and Jayne, now working reduced hours on flexi-time, went to the office till midday. The experiment failed. It meant getting to bed by 9.00pm at the latest and Jayne, mindful of the wrath that would follow any lateness on her part in the morning, would lie awake most nights worrying and end up getting no sleep at all. Chris's problem was different. He finds he can sleep at almost any time, but his body seemed not to be in tune with skating at that hour. He could not get going at all. With Jayne on the verge of tears and sometimes beyond, through the frustration of not being on the top of her form, they gave up the experiment and returned to the comparatively civilised hours of 10.30pm onwards.

The world championships of 1980 at Dortmund provide a collector's item in the form of a serious error by the British couple. At the end of the first day, they lay third behind Linichuk and Karponosov and Regoeczy and Sallay, 'and that was a shock' Jayne declares. For the first time in a championship they had·their noses in front of Moiseyeva and Minenkov. They excelled particularly in the tango romantica, oddly enough a Russian creation of recent years.

The Hungarian judge went as high as 5.8 for Chris and Jayne in this exercise, an extraordinarily high mark for a compulsory dance. They knew they had skated well but were unprepared for a mark like that.

On the second day the computer produced one of those curiosities that mock the attempts of the ISU to find a fair method of establishing results. The British champions just beat Moiseyeva and Minenkov on the kilian—a side-by-side dance—but because the Canadians had secured one fourth place overall Chris and Jayne were relegated to fourth place on a judges' majority. Both the Russian and the British couple were placed third or equal third by five judges and the total of their placed positions have an identical reading, 13 from the two second places (2×2) and the three thirds (3×3). In such circumstances a total of all nine positions is used to break the tie: The Russians had 29 (2×2 plus 3×3 plus 4×4) and the British had 30 (2×2 plus 3×3 plus 3×4 plus 1×5). In terms of overall points, lowest is best. The Canadian judge's preference for her compatriots over Chris and Jayne in fourth place (by 5.4 to 5.3) gave Britain that one telling extra ordinal.

In fact it did not matter because there followed what Jayne calls the fiasco of the original set pattern fox-trot. The 'Little Street in Singapore' seemed to have become a dangerous thoroughfare when Chris and Jayne came to a particular passage in their dance which was usually one of their highlights. At this point in the sequence Jayne wraps her free leg round her partner and leans back while he swings her flamboyantly first one way, then the other. Jayne:

❦ To this day we don't know what happened. I'm still not sure whether I leaned back farther than usual because my left foot—the one on the ice—was slipping, or my foot slipped because I was leaning back too far. There were rumours that there was something on the ice, because we did the very same thing on the second circuit, but we thought not. Certainly it didn't occur to us to have a look at the ice when we had finished. It seemed to me that I did nothing different from the hundreds of other times we'd done that OSP, both in training and competition.

Chris could hardly hold me and he had to go low to prevent me from crashing on the back of my head. It was a difficult step, changing edge as well, but we'd never made a mistake on it before. We didn't miss any steps because of it, didn't even miss the timing. I remember smiling as I came out of it—I always smile when I've done something wrong—but when we did it the second time I didn't smile. A bad mistake is one thing, a bad habit something quite different. I was choked. I can only think there must have been a murphy on the ice. Betty told us afterwards that she died a thousand deaths, so it must have been some howler, because nobody has a more placid disposition. **,**

The third circuit went perfectly and they received a round of sympathetic applause, or perhaps some people recognised a show of character. Jayne goes on: 'When we came off it suddenly hit me what had happened, I was so cross with myself, in a real temper.'

Chris agrees: 'You were, Jayne, in a real temper.' Better perhaps to let her hair down than cry her eyes out, in public at least. On a quick calculation Chris reckoned that they had done that move some 2,000 times in all, without ever making a mistake. Jayne saved the crying ('with temper really') for when she was locked away on her own in the dressing-room and, later still, the hotel room. But it was hard for her to hold back the tears when sympathisers would offer commiserations which were meant kindly but had a cruel effect.

Jayne had recovered her self-control sufficiently to reappear at the rink in the evening to support Robin Cousins when he skated brilliantly in what was his swansong as an amateur. By way of compensation Betty bought Jayne a mink-tail key ring ('the nearest I'll ever get to a mink coat') the next day. Though it undoubtedly was a setback, Betty Callaway saw a silver lining. 'The one thing that came out of it was the way they stood up to a frightening ordeal. Some people might have panicked, or at least let it show and make the rest of the performance second-rate, whereas they skated the whole programme, those two slips apart, exactly as we would have wanted. That showed character.'

At least they were satisfied with their marks in the circumstances. The judges might have been prepared to overlook the first trip, since they had all seen the OSP executed perfectly in practice, but the second trip, more hazardous than the first, clearly called for some penalty and marks ranging from 5.2 to 5.5 were fair. They deprived the British couple, however, of the chance to recover third place. In the end it made no difference because they could not have held the position after the free skating, with Moiseyeva and Minenkov getting marks as high as 6.0 in one case, admittedly from their compatriot on the judging panel. 'But the OSP marks,' Betty Callaway believed, 'showed that the judges were interested in them, if not yet ready to consider them for a medal.'

Their dismay was softened by the victory of their stable-companions, Regoeczy and Sallay. The Hungarians had come close to the Olympic title behind Linichuk and Karponosov and were now willed to the gold medal from second place after the OSP by the enthusiasm of the spectators for them. The judges could hardly have remained unmoved. Perhaps it could not quite take the place of an Olympic title, but at least they were able to leave the scene on a trumphant note, and Chris, Jayne and Betty were happy to share their jubilation.

Chris and Jayne had not allowed the experience of the OSP to affect their free dance. Jayne maintains that she had forgotten about the OSP by the next night; Chris feels that she had subconsciously developed more aggression. Their concern so far as the free was concerned was about the acceptability of the cartwheel with which they brought it to a spectacular finale. Some felt that it would be regarded as illegal and therefore be penalised, but Betty had made soundings and received some sort of assurance that it would be acceptable as being in character with the music, a jive presentation of 'In the Mood'. The cartwheel would be recognised as a finishing pose rather than an acrobatic step within the dance.

Thus ended the most punishing season the British couple had ever experienced and Jayne recalls being 'dog tired' by the end. They had

Chris on duty in Nottingham after qualifying as a police constable (*Nottingham Evening Post Photos*)

competed in three important championships within eight weeks, to follow three other events before Christmas, including the British championship. They had half-expected to be invited to take part in the ISU tour that follows every world championship, but only the first three were chosen, and in time they would have cause to be grateful for that. The tour, as they were to discover the next year and the year after, is no barrel of fun. The first experience is enjoyable and is treasured by those newly arrived at the top but this could wait another year. It can be an exhausting ordeal. In any case, they had no exhibitions strong enough for the company they would keep and they would hardly have been a big success. There was also the question of their jobs to be considered.

Both the police and Norwich Union had to be placated when the chance came to spend five weeks at Oberstdorf, followed by two weeks of ISU summer tour in Europe in 1980. Chris totted up the normal entitlement for holiday that year, added his rest days, calculated how much double time he could claim for rest-day working and Bank Holidays, threw into the equation the days off he would be owed and discovered that the policeman's lot was not so bad after all. He could run up an overdraft of time and pay it off later. For Jayne it was much simpler. She could take her two weeks' holiday and have the rest unpaid. They were venturing into the unknown, but they now see that that summer of 1980 was the turning point in their skating career, and they realised that they had only tapped the surface of their potential.

Home from home in Oberstdorf

Somebody smiled on them from above in the summer of 1980. The outlook was bleak. The Nottingham rink was to close for three weeks for repairs and for much of the rest of the time the ice would be teeming with youngsters on holiday. At best it meant more nocturnal toil, at worst fitting in their training at frenetic public sessions. Then, from out of the blue, came the invitation to Oberstdorf. It was all thanks to Betty Callaway's appeal abroad and loyalty at home. She would go only if her couple could accompany her. No wonder Bernard Ford has called her 'a great lady'. Betty's commitment was for only two weeks, but she arranged for Chris and Jayne to stay for a further three weeks and then go on tour with the ISU. Jayne:

❝When we realised what Oberstdorf had to offer it was like some sort of Shangri-La. We thought it marvellous that we could skate practically as long as we liked, and always at civilised hours. There were few people in the centre, even fewer than now when there are likely to be quite a number of skaters from other countries on a course. At that time there were really only Germans there, so we were very well off. There were only two rinks at the time, but we had about six hours a day on the ice, virtually to ourselves. There was no ballet-room at that time, but we used the weight-training room freely and did a lot of cycling. It seemed like another world to us up there in the Bavarian Alps. We got our programme ready so quickly that we were amazed. Normally it used to take us ages, with the children using the Nottingham rink so heavily at the time we should be putting out programme together.   ❞

The tour took them to Dresden, Karlmarxstadt, Garmisch-Partenkirchen, Davos, Arosa and Hérisau. Being chosen, they thought, was 'a kind of recognition'. The rest of the party included Judy Blumberg and Michael Seibert of the United States, who would be challenging for medals in the wake of Chris and Jayne in the years ahead. But all too soon the dream was over, to be replaced by the nightmare of a crowded rink and a crowded day. Now that they had seen how green the grass was on the other side, below the

Chris, Jayne and Betty at their home from home, outside the ice-skating complex in the Bavarian Alps at Oberstdorf (*All-Sport Photographic*)

daunting heights of the Nebelhorn (fog-horn), they were unwilling to settle for less. They would have to train seriously if they were to have any chance of fulfilling their potential. An hour here and an hour there, and sometimes no hour at all was a depressing prospect, no way to challenge the might of the Soviet Union and hold the United States at bay. All the advantage they had gained from training full-time would now be wasted; they would fall back again. Steadily the idea formed in their minds that they would have to give up work.

For Chris the break came early and easily, for Jayne it was complicated. Indeed, Chris was off the force on 4 August just five days after returning home and with the overdraft of time written off. They were due to take a screening at Richmond that August, which would mean asking for more time off. That would have smacked of impertinence with so much time already owing, and the St Ivel would follow shortly afterwards. Chris:

❝I talked first to a Sergeant Stone, who was a sort of father confessor to me, about how much time I'd had off and how much more I would need to the end of the year. It had already reached thirteen weeks, and I could see that we could not go on like that, however green the grass elsewhere happened to be. I then talked to the Chief Constable and his deputy, who'd always shown interest in my skating. I was in his office for about an hour, quite desperate because I really could not afford not to work, not for long anyway. I explained that this was going to be a big year for us, make or break time, and we'd just about got enough money in the bank to get us through the world championships the following March without my going to work. After that we'd be sunk. He said it was up to me, realising no doubt that in my own mind I would have to leave.

They were prepared to go to any lengths to give me time off, paid or unpaid, and still keep me on the job, but he said in the end he thought the best thing would be to make the break. I'd only been back two days, yet it worked out that I could finish three days later. Normally you have to give two weeks' notice but because of the financial system it just happened I could go much more quickly. It was quite a dramatic and sad moment for me, suddenly out of a job, with no income after six years in one place. It seemed like a good future going down the drain, the uniform I'd been wearing would have to go back. It was a weird feeling because, well, it happened so quickly. All the people that I'd known—I wouldn't get to see them again because some would be on different rosters. Suddenly the job wasn't there any more. I left without having a chance to shake the hands of some of my mates.

Coming out of the room my mind was in a whirl. I had enjoyed police work, something I'd always done. It was going to be my career. I'd lost a lot of security, and yet at the same time I was relieved that the die was cast, that I was being pulled in only one direction now. It would be strange, though, to be on the other, civilian, side of the fence. Jayne couldn't believe it when I told her I'd be finishing in three days. She had known I was going to see the chief but hadn't expected such an abrupt break. **9**

Jayne takes up the story:

6 I wasn't sure he would do it, because I knew it would be a big decision for him. At the same time, I was pleased because it meant that I could leave, too. By now, office work had become a drudgery to me. Also, I'd already been working part-time, so it was no big deal for me. I handed in my resignation the following day, thinking it would be easy, but ... Fancy that, the police can let him go in three days and my place say something like 'You ought to work a month's notice, but we'll let you off with three weeks'. I mean, I wasn't exactly crucial to Norwich Union, the place wouldn't come tumbling to the ground without me. They seemed to be union-oriented, had to do everything by the rule book. A man from the union, ASTMS, had said that if I joined it would be easier to get time off and they would try to get me sponsored by the firm. When I joined nothing happened.

The manager said he thought I was making the right decision, but I suspect he was glad to see the back of me, because I was so often asking for time off and working part-time. When Chris was free, I had to soldier on for two or three weeks more. That was horrible. I couldn't settle down at work at all. I'm sure I didn't do a proper day's work because my heart wasn't in it. I used to work flexi-time, with a key to record when I was on duty. I was supposed to work six hours a day and that would vary according to our training. Even so, I used to fall behind, something like five hours or more. You're allowed to go up to ten hours in arrears before they clamp down. In the end I got so bored I used to take out my key and go for a cup of coffee over the road. I used to do quotations for car insurance, making alterations when people changed their cars. I'd be answering telephone inquiries a quarter of the time. It was no hotbed of commercial activity. **9**

Meanwhile, Chris was looking around for possible sponsors. That was how they hoped to make good the loss of their normal income. But fairy godmothers were thin in the air and it was hardly the time to expect a job that would be compatible with their training, in a sports centre for instance. It was hardly the time to find any job at all in a period of deep recession. Soon Jayne, too, experienced the weird feeling of being unemployed, but they felt their way towards an established training routine at the rink. They skated mainly late at night, from about 10.30pm to 2.00am or whenever they felt like calling a halt, and be up again at about 7.00am for an hour between 9 and 10am.

Many people told them they were mad, others that they were leeches on society, but they never went to sign on at the unemployment office. They did not want to, for a start, since it was their decision to finish work, but in any case they later found out that they would have had to sign a declaration to the effect that they were prepared to take up any suitable employment that was on offer. If they signed that with no intention of doing it 'we'd be committing an offence', Chris says from his former position of law enforcer. They had another chance to go to Oberstdorf at the end of the summer, receiving special terms because they were able to help the German couples. They had already demonstrated some of the compulsory dances under Betty's supervision; now they were often consulted on some problem the other couples might have. In a small way, they were now teachers as well as taught.

Their great year loomed—not that they were to know it. Nor would they be certain which year most fitted that description. In later championships they would attain unprecedented heights, the established stars reaching into some unknown firmament. In the winter of 1980–1 it was the fact of their victories rather than the scale that so stunned the imagination. The possibility of leaping from fourth to first, even after the retirement of Regoeczy and Sallay, belonged in a distant cloud-cuckoo land, the product of someone's fevered imagination. For the moment their target was the St Ivel competition at Richmond in the autumn.

With the disappearance of Robin Cousins from the amateur ranks, Chris and Jayne were the big British names from now onwards. They won well enough at Richmond, as they would have expected to do against opposition that ranked lower than them, but it was not an unqualified success. Their cha-cha OSP did not measure up to their aspirations and the first passage of their free, a jive number to 'Trumpet Blues', fell below standard. The free opening was unready and rushed and, although they felt they could improve it in time for the big challenges which lay ahead, Betty Callaway advised them to find something else. They had been working on an exhibition to music from *Fame* and as it developed they realised it would be ideal for their free opening, with a rock 'n'

With a friend, Clarissa von Lerchenfeld, at a Bavarian evening at Oberstdorf; the Lerchenfeld family have been benefactors in many ways

roll flavour that was something of an innovation. The new free won approval at the British championship that November, but the problem of the OSP remained, to be solved principally by Courtney Jones. He had travelled around, as usual, that summer and seen how much more flamboyantly the Russians and Americans, in particular, were attacking the cha-cha. That would be the weak British link and there was still time to change it. Chris:

❛ He wanted something more vulgar. We needed to throw ourselves at the audience a little more, flaunt ourselves. We'd done the cha-cha on ice, but didn't really know the dance from a ballroom angle. Courtney is strong in ballroom and he took us to a studio and taught us the steps himself. It was more technical than we realised. The strong beats are actually on 'two', much more of a hip movement than anything else. Then Michael Stylianos, a former Latin-American world champion, carried the thing forward in his Top of the Stairs studio at Norbury, south-east London. He showed us the arm movements, which are much more pronounced in that dance than in almost any other, except perhaps for the samba and paso. Betty and Courtney, who had never previously met Mike, watched this with growing interest and the scene then moved to the Richmond rink, where we put Mike's ideas into action to Ted Heath's 'Cherry Pink and Apple Blossom White', not an original choice, I know, but none the less effective for that. It had an unusual opening, more like a paso, that made people sit up expectantly. Another visit to the Top of the Stairs and another to Richmond and we had virtually set it up. ❜

It was during this interlude that they had two strokes of financial fortune. First, the Sports Aid Foundation offered to underwrite their first jobless winter. Their grant was for £8,000, to be taken at intervals leading up to the 1984 Olympics, or as one lump sum at the start. They plumped for the second option, not that it mattered in the end. While the application to the SAF was being considered a Nottingham city councillor walked into the Torvill newsagents' shop, as was his custom, and while his normal business was being transacted he suggested to Betty Torvill that an appeal to the council might fall on sympathetic ears.

The couple did their sums and, armed with an imposing set of figures, attended the council for interview with members of the policy and finance committee. The amount they had hit upon was between £13,000 and £14,000 a year. They had no thought at that time of training anywhere else but at Nottingham. The point needs to be made in the light of subsequent criticisms of their spending much time at Oberstdorf and implications that they were thereby incurring extra cost at the ratepayers' expense. Oberstdorf did not add one penny to the charge on the council.

They left the interview with no clear idea whether or not they had made a favourable impression. True, they were told 'we'll let you know', but there seemed a faint whiff of the deadening 'don't call us, we'll call you'. They were at the house of a friend in Richmond when the bombshell struck. A telephone call from BBC Radio Nottingham asked if they would like to comment on the grant they were to receive from the city council. What grant would that be? The £42,000 they would be getting until the Sarajevo Olympics in 1984.

They were stunned, once they had been assured that it was not somebody's idea of a sick joke. Within £100 or so, this was the precise sum that their researches had led them to believe was their minimum requirement. Suddenly all financial anxiety had fled. Their courage in going out on a limb had been rewarded. A small immediate celebration was followed by a letter of grateful thanks to the council and, in time, the return of a cheque to the Sports Aid Foundation. The couple's answering commitment was to publicise the city, wearing insignia on their clothes so far as it was possible within the amateur rules of the National Skating Association and the requirements of team uniforms.

The grant did not receive unanimous approval in the city and the *Nottingham Evening Post* carried some letters, albeit fewer, expressing dismay as well as support. It became, too, something of a political football. The *Post* of 14 January 1981 carries the following quote from Councillor Jack Green, spokesman for the Tory group: 'The council are already overspent by £12½m on the housing revenue account. I have received several complaints about the grant from ordinary ratepayers. It does seem to be an example of the spend, spend, spend policy of the Socialists.'

The time would come when all criticism would be stilled by performances on the ice which would lift the city spirits and allow the grant to be seen as a worthwhile investment. For every citizen who resented the seven pence a year a head that the grant involved, there would soon be ten others who would willingly pay ten times more, as a matter of civic pride. Later still the mathematics would be academic, since a word of disapproval would be a call to arms for a lynching party.

Returning to Nottingham, their programmes set and their financial problems solved, they found that half the rink had been given over to pantomime practice, so it was not until they went back to Oberstdorf after Christmas that they laid down their cha-cha on a proper rink. They reckon they worked three hours a day on the cha-cha alone, plus another hour or so in the gym. Michael Stylianos went over for five days, not only to provide technical expertise, but also to fuel them further with his zest and enthusiasm. He is the kind of man, Chris says, 'who'll keep going all day, for as long as you like. He'll respond to any suggestions and encourage you to experiment still further.' They went on experimenting until a few days before the European championships in Innsbruck in February 1981, but these were merely refinements to adorn the general picture. But a doubt remained. However much they liked the new creation they had no way of knowing how it would impress the judges. Eventually time ran out and the experimenting had to stop.

During this period Chris began to have trouble with his right leg and was sometimes afflicted by a violent pain. One day he had to go off the ice, but in general he managed to skate through it. He imagined it to be some kind of inflammation but was to learn on returning home that it was a stress fracture—rather more serious. The next trauma concerned their blades at Innsbruck. Jayne:

❛ We were used to the man at Oberstdorf, Heine Podhajsky, a real expert, doing our blades. But his machine was put out of action by a well-meaning cleaner who sprayed it with water, unaware of the damage he would cause. So, panic, panic, we took the risk of an offer at Sonthofen, near Oberstdorf, where a machine of the same type, but older, was installed. The man there cut such a deep hollow in them that they were too sharp and our speed was cut by half. Dance blades are so much thinner than normal blades that you have to have a different way of grinding, a much smaller stone. We persevered with them until we got to Innsbruck where, to our relief, the man from Oberstdorf would be on duty. Even so, it was quite a decision to have the blades done

71

again on the eve of a championship, and with the equipment he had at Innsbruck he still had to play around a bit to get the things right, or at least half-right. We then found them too 'slippy' for comfort, because the hollow was not deep enough and the edge not sharp enough.

Heine Podhajsky, who became a blade specialist because he discovered from his own experiences that there was nobody to fill that important role, recounts an incident that brought home to him the degree of precision that was required. He had ground Jayne's skates to a tolerance of 0.05mm, which is to say that when the blades were vertical it would have been barely possible to slide a sheet of paper less than half the thickness of a British five-pound note under one edge, as he proved on the spot by the use of his micrometer. Yet Jayne ventured only twenty metres or so on to the ice before returning to say the blades were not right. Since then Podhajsky has worked to a tolerance of not more than 0.02mm. That demonstration, together with a ham-fisted attempt of mine to grind a blade at the Slough factory of MK Skates Ltd whose blades Chris and Jayne use, showed me how sophisticated the production of ice-skating blades has become.

Basically three stones are used to hollow-grind the blades and thus produce two distinct edges. For compulsory figures, which do not require sharp edges, a stone of 3in diameter produces an arc that is only just visible to the eye. For free skating and ice dance, however, a much sharper edge is needed and stones to the diameter of 0.875in and 0.75in respectively are used.

The smallest stone is necessary for ice dance as the blades themselves are thinner than those used for free skating, 0.12in compared with 0.15in. The effect of using a free-skating stone on an ice-dance blade is shown in the diagrams (not to scale). Fig 1 shows the free-skating blade and Fig 3 the ice-dance blade, narrower and hollow-ground more acutely (exaggerated here for clarity) by using the stone of smallest diameter. In Fig 2 the dance blade has been ground with a free-skating stone and has a shallower curve and less sharp edges. It will be 'slippy'.

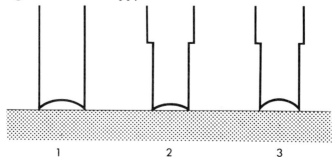

1   2   3

Practice was difficult at Innsbruck because the second rink under a huge bubble was quite unsuitable, 'the worst we've ever known' Jayne insists:

❝It was freezing cold, particularly in the morning and evening, had no atmosphere because of the understandable absence of spectators, allowed water to drip through during the day, when the snow on top melted, and covered an area of bad ice. It was part of a big speed-skating oval and they had put wooden barriers round to define our rink. Somehow it seemed all wrong. There was no provision for spectators and any judges who were prepared to risk pneumonia congregated at one end. This really threw us, since our programme was designed to produce the greatest effect where the judges would sit.

The music was another problem, with the speakers on one side only and echoing on the other, so you could look out of time from certain viewpoints, or maybe unable to hear it at all. Then, our blades were awful. One way and another we felt quite depressed whenever we had to use that bubble rink. The main rink was nice and we quite enjoyed the competition of course! We did the first dance, the Westminster waltz, really well. By that time we had had so many minor irritations, and some not so minor, that we weren't really thinking about which place we would get, only about getting through the thing with our sanity intact. I was stunned when Nicky Slater and Karen Barber came into the women's dressing-room to say 'congratulations, you're first'. I knew we had got good marks but I certainly hadn't realised that they would stand up against all the others. ❞

The second dance was the paso doble, which they skated less well. They had approached it in a different frame of mind from the first. With all the difficulties, they had tackled the Westminster with the sort of resigned determination of 'we've got nothing to lose', whereas with the paso they felt exposed in the lead. They skated more defensively, but it was still a winner. 'What I hated at this stage,' Chris says, 'was people saying congratulations, with so much still to be done. They seemed already to be taking too much for granted.' As for Jayne, she 'wanted to run away and hide, mentally prepare myself for the next day'. But there was no escape. The bottleneck leading to the one door of the stadium ensured that the press would keep a watchful guard. Against their wishes, they said a few inconsequential words to the press (they are not regarded as good copy at the best of times as a result of their natural reserve). Jayne again:

Jayne giving an interview after winning their first European gold medal, at Innsbruck in 1981; note her 'good luck' skate earrings, which she wears at all competitions (*Ice & Roller Skate Magazine*)

❝It is unusual to talk to the press at this stage of a competition, but then I suppose it was an unusual situation, for us at least. We could understand their special interest because it was such a revelation, but you don't want to say how great you feel at this early stage in case you go out again the next day and bomb. Back at the hotel we could feel that the news had got around, 'guess who's in the lead?' A lot of people were pleased for us, and it was nice that some of the Russians, the pair skaters I remember, came up to say 'well done'. But, of course, we knew it wasn't over yet, not by a long chalk, and we fully expected to drop. ❞

That same evening the ice dancers were called for a special practice at the main rink, to eke out what would have otherwise been poor fare for the paying customers with a pathetic entry of only six for the pairs, outnumbered three to two by the judges. Lawrence Demmy, who probably saw this as an opportunity to promote the cause of ice dance, once the Cinderella of the sport, was keen on the idea and, whatever the skaters may have felt about taking part in what amounted to a mini-competition, they would not have wanted to incur official displeasure. All the judges were there, having watched the pairs, and it seemed quite like the real thing. At least it gave the skaters something to do for the evening, rather than sit about and dwell too much on what the morrow might bring.

For Chris 'that was a long, long night; I couldn't wait to get on with the next stage of the competition.' They skipped the following morning's practice, partly because their blades were so 'slippy' and needed nursing and partly because it was scheduled for the bubble rink, always a depressed area for them. No doubt other skaters felt the same, but they could hardly see much consolation in that. It was thoroughly unsuited to the purpose and no amount of fellow suffering could change that situation. Anyway, they knew what they had to do by then and felt no further need for preparation.

The revelations continued. The rumba is a good dance for the British couple 'with a lot of matching lines' of arms, legs and body positions and again they won convincingly. They had three marks of 5.6 and six of 5.7 and every judge placed them first except the Austrian. He could not separate them from Moiseyeva and Minenkov on 5.6. Linichuk and Karponosov, the Olympic champions less than a year earlier, seemed already to be back numbers, with only a bronze medal dangling before them. Chris and Jayne had a bad draw for the OSP cha-cha, second in a field of nineteen, with their principal rivals, Moiseyeva and Minenkov, near the end. Bad, because it is hard for judges to apply the same judgements to two couples separated by as much as an hour and a half in time. It would not matter the following year when their reputation would have been established and judges would have no problem in marking them generously, regardless of whoever would be skating later, but at that time of course they still had a name to make. The rule, anyway, has since been changed so that the starting order for the OSP is decided by positions after the three compulsory set dances.

What with the draw and a general fear that it might all turn out to be too good to be true, they expected—at least Jayne expected—to lose the OSP and perhaps to drop to second overall. But the style that had begun to inform their skating, the combined wisdom of Betty Callaway, Courtney Jones, Bobby Thompson, Michael

Chris and Jayne about to take the first step towards their first international gold medal, the European at Innsbruck in 1981; the first dance was the Westminster waltz (*Colorsport*)

Stylianos and the skaters themselves, exerted a more extrovert, more flamboyant appeal. Their original cha-cha, they feel, may have been more demanding technically, but it was not nearly so expressive. 'There was quite enough difficulty in the new dance,' Jayne explains, 'but with more emphasis on the feeling. We no longer look at the OSP as a compulsory, which strictly speaking it is. It's advanced far beyond that by now. You're supposed to be able to do them in a dance interval. I can never see them doing our OSPs as a compulsory.'

They won the OSP by a less conclusive margin. Six judges placed them first and three, the Swiss and French joining the Russian, gave pride of place to Moiseyeva and Minenkov. But it still exceeded their expectations. In view of the long gap in time between the appearance of the British and Russian couples, Chris had prepared himself for defeat in the cha-cha though he did not share Jayne's gloomy prophecy of declining to second place overall. Pamela Davis, who was not judging that championship, first broke the good news to them, but they hardly dared to look at the marks she displayed before them to dispel their doubts. It was desperately close, with rarely more than a tenth of a mark between them and Moiseyeva and Minenkov either way, not that that was of any great consequence, for when the marks for all four dances were added together the British champions had something to spare.

World champions

If there is any time in a competition that Chris likes best of all, it is at the stage when the compulsories are out of the way (the OSP is a compulsory, though of no fixed pattern) and only the free is to come. They were both now in great heart, no longer feeling that it must be too good to be true, since it is rare for the order to change after the OSP. True, it had happened only the year before when Regoeczy and Sallay took the world championship, but that was an almost isolated incident. But there always seems to be a catch somewhere and the rules for computing the results were changed that year. Previously, the free dance marks were added to the rest and each judge came out with his own order of preference for the whole field. The couple with five first places (a majority out of nine) was the winner. If no couple had five first places there was a tie-break system that took note of second places etc. Under that system Chris and Jayne would surely have been safe, since they led Moiseyeva and Minenkov by 0.9 according to one judge, 0.6 according to another, 0.5 according to a third, and 0.4 according to two others. Barring a British disaster, it would have been impossible for the Russians to have recovered ground to that extent.

Under the new system, however, the compulsories (including the OSP) and the free were treated as separate entities and in the event of a tie the free would be decisive. It was devised (and still is, with further modification) so that the couple in first place scored, or rather suffered, 1.0 point, the couple in second place 2.0, and so on. Assuming now that the other couples were no longer in the running at Innsbruck, a victory for Moiseyeva and Minenkov, by however slender a margin, would have given them 1.0 for the free (and 3.0 overall) and the British 2.0 for the free (and 3.0 overall). In that event the Russians would have been declared the winners because of their superiority in the free. Chris and Jayne could win four of five dances and still be adjudged second. The compulsories would seem to have been irrelevant. Add to all those considerations the fact that Moiseyeva and Minenkov, with their Bolshoi background, always shone in the free and it is easy to understand why the pride of Nottingham (with due respect to Brian Clough and Nottingham Forest Football Club) were prepared for a silver medal after all. At least it would have been better than they had hoped for when they arrived in Innsbruck.

Jayne believes they 'were only trying to soften the blow in case it came. There was no question of negative thinking and we had no intention of giving less than 101 per cent on the night.' Betty Callaway comforted herself with the thought that, with the sudden eclipse of Linichuk and Karponosov, some judges would regard it as a retrograde step to revert to Moiseyeva and Minenkov, who had first won the world championship as long ago as 1975.

Certainly Torvill and Dean had no fears of any couple other than Moiseyeva and Minenkov. Danger would lurk in the years ahead from the third couple, Natalya Bestemianova and Andrei Bukin, but they were comparatively unknown in 1980. Linichuk and Karponosov were a sad case. World champions in 1978 and 1979 and Olympic champions in 1980, they had lost the world title to the Hungarians after Lake Placid and were now clearly seen by the judges as inferior to two other couples. They had virtually dropped from first to fourth within twelve months. Time would show that there would be no place for them in the Soviet Union's team for the world championships at Hartford, Connecticut, a month later.

On the afternoon before the free the British champions whiled away the time in Jayne's room. Chris was glad not to be in a single room in Innsbruck, because he felt the need for some company. He was sharing with Stephen Williams, the male half of the third British couple, who is as untidy in arranging his clothes and things as Chris is fastidiously correct. 'It's not the time when you want to be totally alone,' Chris says. 'You need somebody around, somebody to talk to occasionally, but not somebody who'll go nattering on about skating. You need some sort of light relief. The skating is on your mind already, so you want a little flippant chat to divert the attention.'

Stephen Williams and Wendy Sessions, his partner, fit the pattern well, especially Wendy, and it was fortunate that she was sharing a room with Jayne. Chris and Stephen passed the afternoon in the girls' room with Wendy holding court in her Birmingham accent for most of the time and lapsing into quiet reflection at others, since she and Stephen were facing almost as big a test, their first free dance in the European championships. A year later Chris would have his own room at Lyons for the next Europeans and 'not care for it one bit'. The day wheeled slowly by in Innsbruck, with the population of the hotel steadily declining. Those not involved in ice dance would have left early for the rink to secure their places and the competitors would successively depart for the rink as the time approached for them to appear. Eventually only those in the last group would be left, nervously trying not to cross each other's path, to avoid the embarrassing civilities that would follow.

The Nottingham couple's routine is to leave the hotel in time to

Britain make a clean sweep at the St Ivel competition at Richmond in 1981; on the left are Wendy Sessions and Stephen Williams, with Karen Barber and Nicky Slater on the right (*All-Sport Photographic*)

arrive about an hour and a half before they are due to skate. They make for their respective changing-rooms, hoping against hope that the places they have claimed all week will still be vacant, the clothes' pegs uncluttered. If Chris's are not he will be tempted to shift somebody else's belongings. 'Generally speaking, when you are in a more senior position you can move people about, pull a bit of rank, but in fact it rarely happens once you have staked your claim at the start of the week.' Jayne is not so assertive: 'I freak out if someone gets my place.' In Lyons the following year Jayne and Irina Moiseyeva, her principal rival, would find themselves much too close for comfort as they prepared to do battle.

Chris and Jayne will now go for something to drink, invariably tea for Jayne and probably coffee for Chris. Jayne will drink her tea in a position where she can watch some of the skating, probably Wendy and Stephen, then she will find a quiet area for some exercises, bending and stretching anything that will bend or stretch without too much discomfort. Chris will be somewhere else (they hardly see each other between the time they arrive and the time for them to skate), drinking a little, watching a little. Both like to see a

bit of the competition and soak up the atmosphere. Time drags.
Chris:

❝ At Innsbruck I remember I had about twenty minutes to kill between
all the preliminary preparations and being called to the ice. It was
awful. I wanted to relax, but I found I was going through the whole
programme step by step in my mind about every minute. With
experience I now find I can put it out of my mind a little. I didn't
then, nor do I now, want to talk to anybody and when I leave the
dressing-room I tend to look at the floor or into the distance, so as to
avoid catching anyone's eye. That would probably mean exchanging
a few words and I certainly don't want that. ('He doesn't even talk
to me,' Jayne interjects.) I'm told I have a glassy, far-away look in
my eyes at these times, but I wouldn't know. The tension, even after
years of experience, is tremendous. I wonder how boxers feel before
going out to a world title fight? They're facing a good hiding as well. ❞

Jayne, unlike Chris, will have changed into a tracksuit for her tea
and peeped into the rink. Now she will go back to the dressing-room
to get ready for action. The left boot, as with Chris, has to be laced
up first, and soon enough she will be ready for the dance in all her
colourful glory. They were the couple in maroon in 1981. The
earrings are in place, the hair newly lacquered, the face freshly made
up, the whole immaculately groomed, even to black nail varnish on
the soles of her boots. The three 'paddy bears' will keep silent watch

Jayne with her three 'paddy bears'
(*Christopher Dean*)

within her skating bag, as yet unadorned by the ribbons of victory—the first less than an hour away.

Chris, too, has had to go through the 'yukky' ordeal of make-up. He does so only for the major championships and big television exhibitions—the lights and the reflections from the ice give everyone a deathly pallor. Then he will be back in his room to get dressed, starting of course with the left boot. The men's dressing-room is a more tranquil retreat than the women's. The men tend to vanish soon after they have skated, whereas the women hang around, either in tears or ecstasy according to how they have performed, or at least how they have been marked. A hint of hysteria is never far away.

However well she has skated, Wendy will be certain to let her hair down. 'I've finished, I've finished' she will cry, probably stretched out on the floor in utter relief. Jayne and Karen Barber, the music still to be faced, are a little envious. The men sometimes intrude on the ladies and that will add to the numbers and the noise. There is no prudery here. 'The Russian girls are the ones,' Chris declares. 'They're always walking about in the nude.' Betty Callaway will be sure to look in at one point to make sure that all is well.

Back in the men's dressing-room Andrei Minenkov will be going through a rigorous routine, flat out for a quarter of an hour until he is running with sweat. Most other men have some sort of work-out, but again Chris tends to stand apart. Save for a little bending and stretching, more to relieve nervous tension than anything else, he does nothing. 'I feel worse if I'm too loose,' he says. 'I prefer to be a little tighter to start with.' By now the last couple in the previous group will have started their dance and it is time to go into action.

Chris will meet Jayne outside, or perhaps in a passage leading to the rinkside, or at the rinkside itself. No word will pass, no touching of hands, no apparent recognition of the other. Jayne may find that the laces she had so carefully tied in the dressing-room mysteriously need adjustment. Betty will be hovering around, but not right on top of her pupils. The previous skaters come off and a stampede of the last group for warm-up will start, preceded in one instance by meticulous attention to the placing of the skate guards.

The warm-up over, Chris and Jayne have a quarter of an hour or so to kill. Moiseyeva and Minenkov skate first and in the dressing-room Chris stands with his hands clapped tightly to his ears. At all costs he does not want the marks to penetrate his consciousness. Jayne has her face clasped in her hands, more concerned to dredge up the last ounce of concentration. Moiseyeva, her duty done, slips back to put on her tracksuit and Jayne notes with some inner dismay that her face is aglow. Bad news, it seemed, but in fact the Russian couple's marks had left them vulnerable. They got as high as 5.9 for artistic impression, as one might have expected, but their technical merit marks averaged only 5.75.

The door was open, though Jayne was not to know it, and she remembers being unnerved when she rejoined Chris at the rinkside by the sight of Moiseyeva sitting comfortably between her husband and her trainer, Lyudmila Pakhomova, apparently without a care in the world. An eternity, it seems, has passed before they are at last back on the ice, listlessly tracing tiny circles together while the judges deliberate on the previous couple, Bestemianova and Bukin. Eventually their names are called and they glide to the spot they have chosen for the start of their free dance. Suddenly, as if by royal command, the applause dies and they take up their position. Jayne takes up the story:

‘This is the worst time of all, the couple of seconds before the music starts.. It may seem not much more than the blink of an eye but time seems to stand still as you wait and wonder if something might go wrong. It is important to us to catch the very first note at full concentration, because we always like to explode with a bang to create an immediate impact. As the split seconds tick away, you're consumed with a thousand doubts. You think, what if the tape's got stuck, what if I don't move at the beginning, what if I fall over, what if someone makes an unexpected noise and one of us is startled into moving before the other? The alternative, of course, it to allow a few notes to pass before going into action, but that always seems less dramatic to us. It really is a nerve-racking moment or two, even makes me nervous to think about it months afterwards.’

Their programme that year was composed of a modern jazz dance from *Fame*, an Egyptian-type routine to the music of ‘Caravan’, a slow, seductive rumba to a ‘Red Sails in the Sunset’ that Vera Lynn would never have recognised, and a swinging finale to, appropriately, ‘Swing, Swing, Swing’. Each piece had a different character and the highlights in each were all quite different from each other and from anything they had done before. At that time it was customary for some couples to repeat a section from a previous free programme. The British champions have never subscribed to that practice, even to the extent of discarding individual moves perfected over many hours of training. That philosophy would reach its apotheosis with the revolutionary *Mack and Mabel* the following winter, a programme which would set a standard that others would have to struggle to emulate. They look back on their Innsbruck, and subsequently Hartford, programme as dated and disjointed, as indeed it is in an era of *Mack and Mabel, Barnum* and *Bolero*, but it was bang up to date at the time, perhaps even before its time in the swing section with a rock 'n' roll OSP to come two years later.

It went perfectly. Their only small doubt was that the first section might be too demanding physically, to which Jayne added a further personal little worry about a particularly strong edge she had to hold at one tight corner. But their programme went with such a zing that Jayne could not even remember afterwards skating the sharp corner that had so troubled her in anticipation. Looking back, they both feel that they skated as well as they could possibly have done, at that time at least, and they struck their finishing pose in a mood of exhilaration. The marks were still to come but a feeling of total fulfilment took possession of them, whatever the judges might subsequently decide. Given the pressure they were under as leaders in the competition and on the first occasion of such eminence, it spoke volumes for their character that they should rise to the occasion so triumphantly. Jayne again:

‘Betty was there to greet us when we came off, quietly happy for us and herself as we could see, but it is not in her nature to jump around. 'Well done,' she said, just that. When the marks came up we were still not sure who'd won. Usually you can tell, one way or the other, but we weren't aware of the general level of Moiseyeva's and Minenkov's marks, let alone whether five of the nine judges had remained faithful to us. Betty thought our marks were better, but wasn't sure and went off to find out. In the meantime Carol Heiss, five times a former world champion for the United States and now working in television, came up to give us the good news. Seven judges placed us first in the free, the Hungarian gave us identical marks and the Russian alone preferred Moiseyeva and Minenkov. The Russian alone, again, placed us second overall to his own couple. In fact, we'd won well. I felt like crying, but not until I escaped to the shelter of the dressing-room. Chris maintains that he did not shed a few tears, but I have my doubts. We were both under a highly emotional charge and needed some release. ’

Chris's evidence is that he was now 'bubbling' and no longer feared coming face to face with any old acquaintance and having to make conversation. Let the world come and he would now be happy to look them full in the eye—but not, preferably, the world's press.

Chris and Jayne 'Swing, Swing, Swing' to their first world title at Hartford, Connecticut, in 1981 (*Ice & Roller Skate Magazine*)

He and Jayne had little to say for themselves and were relieved, if anything, to see that the press for the most part cast their ammunition at the Russian couples. The demise of Linichuk and Karponosov, the Olympic champions now placed third in Europe, and the less dramatic decline of Moiseyeva and Minenkov were obviously subjects of much interest. Here was a rare chance for western journalists to delve into their background, so far as that was possible through deadpan interpreters. There was a poignant moment when Linichuk and Karponosov, so suddenly knocked off their pedestal, announced their retirement. They were married soon afterwards.

The only significant question addressed to the new champions concerned the council grant, a political minefield for them to negotiate in their first press conference. Jayne felt 'quite depressed' afterwards, and would have much preferred to return to their hotel straight away to join in the celebrations that would already have begun. They were, they admit, out of their depth compared with the others who were all old hands, and they were content to let Betty handle the most difficult questions. But before then came the medal ceremony. Jayne:

❝ This was very moving. In her autobiography Sophia Loren has said that she always felt as if she were someone else watching a celebrity from a distance. That's how it seemed to me on that podium. Perhaps a lot of people in the public eye feel that, that they're outside looking in when a big thing happens to them and they're subjected to a lot of publicity. Perhaps it's nature's way of helping you to overcome nerves and stress. You feel that it's not really happening to you. You're watching someone else you know quite well, a close friend perhaps. All the same it was definitely Jayne Torvill who felt terribly proud when the Union Jack climbed the centre flagpole, flanked by two subsidiary hammers and sickles. I was conscious for the first time during the week that millions of people at home would be watching this on television at home. I hope it does not sound conceited but I felt that I'd done something not just for myself but for my country, with all those people in the stadium honouring our flag. There were no tears, but I felt as if I was crying with joy inside. ❞

A telegram from Robin Cousins was a treasured possession among the many messages of congratulation that flowed into their hotel, almost from the moment they arrived back there that night. But first, yet another formality had had to be negotiated, the dope test. Chris was surprised to discover that it was 'quite a nice time'.

World champions for the first time—
on the victory podium at Hartford,
1981 (*All-Sport Photographic*)

With competition over, everyone was suddenly relaxed and ready for a laugh, which came easily under the strain of producing a urine specimen against the body's instincts. There is rarely any display of small-mindedness, of the losers allowing possible bitterness or envy to show through.

The men generally drink beer to help the bladder out and 'get quite stoned', according to Jayne. Chris explains that after a long period of comparative abstinence in pursuit of perfect physical conditioning 'it goes straight to your head'. A cola was enough for Jayne. In neither case, of course, was there any trace of an illegal substance in their system. The glow remained with Jayne the next morning, but Chris's spirits had dropped:

❛I felt flat with anti-climax, having to reappear at the rink early for exhibition practice after a late night. Giving exhibitions are not always the bundle of fun they might appear, especially those that are required at championships. By then you've done so much skating that you're drained. On television it's always explained that this is the time, with competition over, when skaters can relax and let their hair down. But exhibitions can be really hard work and if you don't skate well people are apt to curl their lip and say that the champions are nothing great, especially if they haven't seen us in the actual competition. ❜

Jayne, in general, would agree but on this occasion she 'still felt on a high and wanted to carry on skating.' In fact, they produced such sparkling exhibitions that an English voice was heard to cry: 'We won the exhibitions, too.' There could be no doubt that Chris and Jayne were the most popular of the three medal-winning couples on show after the women's free skating the following evening. English patriotic fervour was understandable in view of the famine that Britain's ice dancers had suffered during a decade of Russian domination. During the traditional Sunday show that followed the championships Chris and Jayne were asked to close the afternoon, an honour certainly but submitting them to the ordeal of following three other European champions. That had to bear comparison with such crowd-pleasing skaters as Igor Bobrin, a gifted Russian comic when it came to exhibitions, and Denise Biellmann, a beautiful and acrobatic Swiss. Their newly won reputation held.

They left Innsbruck with happy memories, to be greeted at Heathrow by the mayor of Nottingham and various representatives of the media, one of whom resumed the insensitive, as they believe, question of their support from the council. Jayne fobbed him off with some non-committal reply, although pointing out that their grant would not come from additional rates. They did not feel it was a subject for public discussion in this casual fashion, if at all, so far as they were concerned. The decision to make the grant lay elsewhere and the question should be raised elsewhere. Another sour note was contained in a report from the *Nottingham Evening Post* on 7 February 1981. It read:

❛A please-come-home-and-spend-your-ratepayers'-money-here plea was made to the couple today by their first coach, Mrs Janet Salisbury, who as Janet Sawbridge was herself an outstanding skating champion. Mrs Salisbury, of Cinder Hill, said: 'What Jayne and Chris have done is marvellous, a Cinderella story, a great achievement. But I wonder whether it is a Nottingham victory or a German victory. Things seem to have turned a little topsy-turvy in that Nottingham ratepayers' money is going to help them train in Germany. They have given up their jobs and this has obviously paid off in both ways. But they have not won the European championship in six months' work. I sensed as soon as they got together that they would be champions and I believe they will be the next Olympic champions. But if they came home now, rather than train in Germany, they would not need money to the excessive amount that they need for living expenses over there. I think they could get whatever training facilities they want in this country, especially now that they don't have to fit in training with their jobs.'

And Councillor Jack Green, Conservative group leader on the city council, said: 'Of course they should be congratulated on their success, but I would ask that they now consider coming home to Nottingham. First this would save the ratepayers' money, as they would not need such high living expenses as in Germany, and secondly I agree with Mrs Salisbury that they should be able to get ice time locally without any problems.'

After becoming the first Britons for twelve years to win the European ice dance trophy, Jayne said: 'We have had a lot more time to prepare and obviously this has given us a lot more confidence. We have been able to go abroad to use facilities, but we also have good facilities in Nottingham and we will be back soon.' Chris said: 'From the first day we arrived in Innsbruck and started training we knew we had to go on the ice and do a faultless performance every time. This was over something like seven days so it became quite difficult as the tension began to mount.' He was convinced that going into full-time training with the backing of the city council had been an advantage. 'In the past few days the benefits of full-time training have made a tremendous difference to us. We can contend now with the best in the world—and we've proved it by winning for Nottingham and for Britain,' he said. **9**

The criticism was on two levels: that ratepayers' money could be better used for general purposes and that it should be used in this country, preferably in Nottingham. Obviously it is a matter of opinion whether the money could be better used, but the success that Chris and Jayne achieved must have had some beneficial effect on the city of Nottingham, whose name and motif they carried prominently displayed on tracksuit and tee-shirt. Is it more proper to make a grant, say, to a gifted violinist or architect than to those whose talents lie in a sporting field—a field incidentally that receives world-wide publicity and brings the city to the attention of millions.

It would have been helpful if Mr Green and Janet Salisbury had followed up his remark that 'they should be able to get ice time locally without any problems' with some concrete proposal. Pious hopes do not produce world champions. As for using the money in a foreign country, Chris and Jayne have some sympathy for that point of view and would have avoided it had there been a viable alternative. Unfortunately, there was none, at least not one that allowed them the opportunity to explore their talents to the full unless they were prepared to skate through the night. Some skaters have to live like owls, but none would do so if there was any way of avoiding it. As it was, the unsocial hours that Chris and Jayne had been prepared to keep surprised their friends. Jayne:

❝Whenever we were invited out and at some stage offered a drink we used to have to explain that we'd rather not because we would be going on to the rink to train. They would be incredulous, because this would be about nine or ten in the evening. We'd say that we wanted to start training at about eleven and they'd say we must be mad. Then, when we started going to Oberstdorf, incidentally for never more than six or seven weeks at a time, some people seemed to think that would be great fun for us, but it's hard, hard work. It's no holiday.   ❞

Indeed, it is not, as I can readily confirm. My abiding memory of one trip to Oberstdorf in pursuit of the Torvill and Dean story proves the point. I was slinking away one dripping morning to catch the train for Munich. It was about seven o'clock and the street and station were largely deserted. It was raining again—it had been a miserable summer there—and the village was either still at slumber or trying to summon up the resolve to get up and face yet another depressing day. Before I left I peeped into the rink, again deserted except for two dedicated figures, even at that hour, going through their paces on the smallest of the three rinks under one roof.

They were tracking their every movement in a mirror running the whole width of the rink. Any imperfections would be revealed and a movement would be repeated time and time again until it gave total satisfaction. This session would last an hour and a half, and would be followed by three more during the day. In what might be laughingly called spare time Chris and Jayne would probably be in the ballet-room practising new moves on the floor. Some holiday. They discovered that six weeks or so in a claustrophobic, if often beautiful, environment were as much as they could take before homesickness set in. Nottingham had no cause to feel deserted in any way.

Janet Sawbridge may have had some acquaintance with Oberstdorf from early days, but her ignorance of what the village now had to offer, on generous terms, is obvious from the absurd comparison she makes. Could any city in Britain provide six hours of ice time a day, at a reasonable hour and often on an empty rink, or a rink with a mirror running across its width, or a complex that provides also a ballet room, sauna, swimming pool, accommodation and restaurant—all under one roof? The occasional switch to Oberstdorf did not add to the city's burden, since the original estimate submitted by Chris and Jayne was made before any question of going to Oberstdorf came about. Far from proving a costly adventure, it gave marvellous value for money—and produced results. They felt a little hurt and a little angry and were at first inclined to make a public reply, but when their anger and hurt had subsided they judged it to be inadvisable. Chris was resigned to the fact that 'whenever you come into the public eye, in whatever capacity, you're bound to get fors and againsts.' A telegram of congratulations from the then Minister of Sport, Mr Hector Monro, belonging to the same party as Mr Green, provided an ironical postscript to the whole business.

They were saddened by Janet's part in political manoeuvrings. In some other person they might have dismissed it as an expression of jealousy, aroused by their having achieved success without her assistance, but that was not the Janet Sawbridge they had known. She was simply not made that way, even though she must have been aware, as they were, of the cloud that hung over their parting. Neither side had made any effort to contact the other, which suggests no love lost between them. One is surprised that they could fall out with anyone, in view of the correctness of their behaviour and the serenity of their characters. The rift with Janet is the only blot on an otherwise blameless record, not that they were necessarily to blame for that. Nowhere else in the field of skating, domestic or international, have I met anyone who has an ill word to say of them. Perhaps it is the one wart I am seeking in order to present them as something other than paragons of virtue, almost too good to be true. Perfection can pall.

Chris returned home to a new crisis. Jayne claims that it saw him at his long-suffering worst:

❝ We were doing a television programme, *Ace Report*, with the swimmer Sharron Davies one day in Nottingham and Chris slipped away to consult a specialist about his leg. It had troubled him occasionally during training in Innsbruck but not during competition, when I suppose he was deep in concentration. By the time he got back we were at lunch with a place saved for him, everybody in high spirits. Chris immediately threw a damper on everything. Laurence Olivier could not have done it better. He put on this solemn, dramatic face and said: "I won't be able to skate this afternoon. I've got a stress fracture." No, he did not just say it, he announced it. I wonder he did not get the towncrier in to do it for him. I could have killed him—I was so embarrassed.

With those TV people around it would be in the *News of the World* the following Sunday, and we were due to go to Hartford for the worlds in a couple of weeks' time. We had expected to be finished by lunch, but they wanted us back on the ice in the afternoon after the figure patch. We did not want to, but they were so persuasive that it was hard to refuse. Then Chris comes back and there is a big depression, 'cos Chris has got a stress fracture. I know it was horrible for him, but it was the way he said it. I could have crawled under the table. If it had been me, I would have broken the news quietly and gradually let it out. But at least he had something to be depressed about. After a quick trip to Oberstdorf, we came home a day early for Chris to see a specialist at Harley Street and he confirmed the stress fracture. **9**

When they reached Hartford, Connecticut, for the world championships of 1981 they trained at half throttle, leaving the ice as soon as there was any slight pang in Chris's leg. In any case training at a championship, according to Chris, is only 'show time'—an opportunity to condition the judges in your favour before battle begins, rather than to slog away at possible weaknesses. Those are best hidden. Skaters who have a weakness tend to disregard it and hope everything will be all right on the night. During the 1976 Olympics at Innsbruck some skaters motored to Garmisch-Partenkirchen, several hours away in West Germany, in order to avoid prying eyes. The practices went well for Chris and Jayne, with their blades less troublesome than in Innsbruck so that they could vanish quite quickly without arousing suspicion. Only Betty Callaway and Joan Wallis, the team leader, knew their dark secret.

The championships began with the paso doble, their weakest dance in Innsbruck, so much so that they had been advised by Lawrence Demmy to work on it. They skated near the end when the ice was rutted, and they opted for caution rather than bravura. Although the American press could not see beyond their anti-Russian prejudices to the real threat from Europe, the British couple were only too aware that those who knew their skating would be studying them as European champions and therefore favourites for Hartford. Even so, they won the paso doble well from Moiseyeva and Minenkov, by seven judges to one with one shared. The rumba was a different matter. Although three judges marked them level with the Russian couple, they felt in their own minds that theirs was a fine exercise and helped to dispel any doubts that might have lingered from the paso. Jayne comments:

6 The rumba is a hard dance, but good for us if we manage to get a lot of matching free legs and lines, one of the main things about the dance. The French judge, Lysiane Lauret, gave us 5.9 which was almost unheard of in a compulsory. By the next day we had begun to worry about our blades again, or at least Chris had. The team had gone to the States early to offset possible jet lag and our skates, in spite of abbreviated practices, were beginning to feel the strain. We hadn't had them sharpened because you don't let any Tom, Dick or Uncle Sam touch your blades. We didn't feel we could trust anybody at Hartford. Chris was really worried and complained during the Westminster that his blades felt quite slippy. **,**

Even so, they were in great form and won this dance even more convincingly. Apart from a tie with Moiseyeva and Minenkov according to the Russian judge, they made a clean sweep. Their matching rise and fall is particularly striking in a waltz and adds point to the explanation given by Pamela Davis as one of the ingredients of their success. She says:

❝Where they are so good is that their depth and length of edge are the same. If you just watch their heads you will see that they rise and fall at exactly the same moment. You can get a boy doing a bigger lobe [curve] and the girl doing a smaller one, but here, if you watch the drawing on the ice, it's the same. And that's where their technique is so good. All the time you're doing a compulsory dance, you're doing lobes, weaving down the rink. It's just an edge, and turning into a turn for the next edge. They're doing their edges absolutely together.
If you've got a girl cutting in and a boy doing a wider movement, you see their heads are not together. The deeper edge takes them farther out, covering more ice. To some extent it's a matter of luck when two skaters match like that. They started off matching well and it's developed over the years into a remarkable togetherness. They were compatible, and that's why they've improved so quickly. Similarity of thought, edge and timing were there from the beginning, but don't think it's all a matter of luck. I've never seen a couple work with such dedication as Chris and Jayne. **,**

They won the OSP from Moiseyeva and Minenkov by six judges to three, yet they felt that they skated better than at Innsbruck, as a result of several more weeks to hone it into shape. Madame Lauret, who had given them 5.9 for the Westminster waltz as well as the rumba, now preferred the Russians to the Britons but she still had Chris and Jayne first overall, as did all nine judges, even Igor Kabanov, of the Soviet Union. As for the free, Jayne reports:

❝It was definitely better than at Innsbruck, because we skated out more. We were drawn first, so that put us off a bit and we thought we might have better luck when there was a redraw because of a mistake, but every couple in the last group drew the same place. We have this ambivalent attitude to draws. We like to get on with it instead of fretting in the dressing-rooms, but it is clearly an advantage to go last so far as the marks are concerned. Moiseyeva and Minenkov had that advantage at Hartford. I was alarmed when Chris went off the ice after one circuit of the warm-up and wondered what new drama was in store. All that had happened was that he had stepped on to the ice with the right foot, ie the wrong one, and had to start again. Betty said that for one horrible moment she thought that his leg had 'gone'. But it stood up and so did our Innsbruck routine, with a bit more authority this time. We got a marvellous reception. The atmosphere was fantastic, with the ice dance held till the last night and the stadium filled to the rafters with 15,000 spectators. When we came off I got changed into my track-suit and went for a stroll in the shopping mall that forms part of the Hartford Civic Center Coliseum. I wanted to get away from it all for twenty minutes, to lose myself among strangers while the others skated. **,**

Chris went through his normal routine of excommunication, sitting in the dressing-room without moving a muscle, his senses obliterated so far as that was possible. At one point he was aware of a huge, collective gasp in the rink and later learnt it had been evoked by a fall by the American couple, Blumberg and Seibert, a mistake that almost certainly caused them to lose third place to the second Russian couple, Bestemianova and Bukin. Moiseyeva and Minenkov brought down the curtain with a performance that lacked their usual

The winners' press conference at Hartford with their delighted trainer; Chris and Jayne, now sponsored by the City of Nottingham, wear the appropriate insignia on their tracksuits (*Ice & Roller Skate Magazine*)

sparkle; the marks of Torvill and Dean, marks of nine 5.9s and nine 5.8s, may have taken the wind out of their sails. They would have needed a string of 6.0s to overtake the British couple. When Chris and Jayne reappeared separately at the rinkside there was a curious lack of interest, a prime example of British understatement carried to an extreme. Nobody rushed up to congratulate them, Joan Wallis nodded at them non-committally, Betty seemed not the least elated. Had they not won, then?

To this day they cannot remember how they came to learn of becoming world champions for the first time. Jayne recalls Betty coming into the dressing-room a little later to say 'well, we did it ducks'—a colloquialism so strangely out of character as to suggest a release from tension. The new champions both felt flat, for which Chris offers the explanation that 'there had been a lot of tension and that had played on us a lot. The first time we had won was a big scene, but the second time, at Hartford, was a pressure thing. Maybe people didn't look at it like that, said we'd have nothing to lose. If only they'd known!' To which Jayne adds: 'You do feel drained after worlds. I mean in 1982 I was just about cracking up. It had been a long month and a half between the start of the Europeans and the end of the worlds.'

There was a huge pile of mail awaiting them when they returned home, but that would not be for several weeks, because they were now prominent members of the ISU touring company up and down North America. They got a little depressed about the tour once the initial excitement had abated. They felt isolated, with the group otherwise split into Americans and Canadians, Russians and a few East Germans. Jayne missed Betty, who had returned home, and was deprived of the company of Debbie Cottrill, the British champion, who had finished fourth in Hartford and been invited to tour. She declined on the ground that her exhibitions were not strong enough for that company.

In Nottingham they now received a great deal of recognition in the streets, at a civic reception and on television and radio. There was nothing in the press now about the questionable use of public funds, either because their opponents had retreated in disarray or because a new fuss had blown up over the expenditure of £60,000 on a mosaic outside the council offices. They particularly appreciated the tribute which came from Nottingham Forest, suggesting that their success had removed the disappointment felt in the city over the loss of the European Cup soccer title.

The magic of
Mack and Mabel

In the spring of 1981, Chris and Jayne had barely returned from the ISU tour before they were considering ideas for the following season. They had to create an OSP to a blues rhythm, an OSP that would stand out from the pack, and a new free programme that would reveal a substantial advance on anything they had done before—not in obedience to the dictates of the ISU, of course, but to satisfy their own self-respect. They were to succeed to such an extent that the coming season would show them as stunning innovators as well as brilliant technicians.

They had a tape taken from an LP they had found in the library of BBC Radio Nottingham. The library is about ten yards square, crammed with shelf after shelf of LPs, a daunting prospect in which to find something at random that might suit their purpose. But they had developed a short cut. They could now drop the recording needle on a track and know within a couple of spins of the turntable whether or not it would be any good. On two previous occasions they had tinkered with the idea presented by an LP whose first attraction (to Jayne, as it happened) was nothing more than the scarlet splash on its sleeve. It is sometimes like that, she explains. A striking cover can arouse a subconscious suspicion of something striking inside, 'and yet another can be so boringly dull that you are intrigued to know what the music is like'.

They had considered this particular record for the 1979–80 season and again the following year, but although it had made some general appeal they had not been sure what to do with it. With their growing expertise now came a growing awareness of their capabilities and this third time they went to the extent of securing a tape in order to consult Betty Callaway and various friends whose opinions they valued. Eventually it was to turn out to be a dazzling success. It was Jerry Herman's *Mack and Mabel*, a Broadway show woven round the tempestuous love affair between Mack Sennett, tyrannical master of the silent movies before the First World War, and Mabel Normand, his leading lady. Side by side with this development was the birth of a blues that was scarcely less stunning. In precise chronological order the blues came first. Chris:

‘We were all quite adamant that it should be completely different from anything the others might offer. We tried to think of the obvious thing and go the opposite way, so we came up with the idea of going back to the roots, a sort of sad lament rather than an upbeat sexy blues. We had no clear vision of the music at that time, except that it should be a strong single instrument. Someone suggested it ought to be an unusual instrument—something like a harp, I think, he had in mind. But a few months beforehand I'd seen a Michael Parkinson programme on television in which Larry Adler was a guest and he'd played a great harmonica with a violonist. That memory remained with me and the next day we went to the Nottingham library and pulled out a Larry Adler LP.

The track that most appealed to us both was Gershwin's 'Summertime', very striking and evocative. Our main doubt was that it was so well known that somebody else might use it. Choosing a piece of music is fraught with the same difficulty as a woman choosing a hat. We experimented with other music and other instruments, but we kept coming back to Larry Adler and 'Summertime'. Our minds were finally made up by the strong sound the record made over the system at the rink.　　　**9**

The work of creating a dance had still to be done, but the choice of music is at least half the battle and over the next weeks and months they came to fashion a blues whose beauty and haunting appeal to the senses would reduce spectators to tears in the season ahead. In choosing the slowest tempo allowed by the ISU they had imposed a special discipline on themselves, since all the movements—deprived of the excitement of pure speed—had to be unusually interesting to look at without being merely attractive for their own sake. 'We didn't want just pretty lines,' Jayne says. It was a difficult exercise of the mind as well as the feet.

Some idea of the dedication they showed is provided by what appeared to be a simple, slinky movement of the knees towards the end of each circuit. It occupied only two or three seconds of the dance, yet they had to spend two hours one day mastering the move, since the change of edge was deceptively difficult. 'Imagine skating round for two hours,' Jayne says, 'doing the same edge and arguing about it. Perhaps we are crazy after all!' They spent an hour one night perfecting their dramatic finishing pose, where Jayne lies despairingly across Chris's back. Jayne:

6Jon Lane, a teacher from Streatham, happened to be at Oberstdorf at the time and watched us developing that move from the seclusion of the restaurant with growing frustration as each successive adjustment we made failed to work before finally everything suddenly clicked into place. He was a spectator at the rinkside on another occason when we were making up a programme and I kept

97

A soulful moment during practice for their 'Summertime' blues OSP (*All-Sport Photographic*)

falling until we got the move right. He overheard someone in a group of non-skating spectators remark: 'That's what happens when beginners get above themselves.' But, with some of the stuff we do, you can look like raw beginners until you get it right. **,**

There were seven or eight highlights in each circuit of the OSP, but they did not want it to look like that, so every highlight had to proceed to the next one with an interesting series of steps or lines. It had to look like one whole devastating highlight. At that stage it was somewhat rough-cut. The full impact would come when the steps were totally mastered and they could apply themselves to the presentation. Betty Callaway would then watch spectators rather than her pupils to gauge the effect, having impressed on them the need to create an atmosphere, to touch people's hearts.

Meanwhile a disagreement developed between Chris on the one hand and Jayne and Betty on the other over the use of *Mack and Mabel* as a single entity spanning the whole four minutes of their free programme. The two women were keen to incorporate the rumba the British couple now use as an exhibition, but Chris remained as faithful to *Mack and Mabel* as Sennett had rarely been to his partner. Jayne now recognises that using the rumba would have been 'a stupid mistake'.

Nevertheless the rumba was still there when they started putting the programme together at Oberstdorf in the summer and receded only reluctantly as *Mack and Mabel* took an ever-stronger hold on the two skaters' imaginations. Chris had the early inspiration of setting the opening against a background of melodrama, with the ogre pursuing the helpless damsel. Jayne had her doubts because she was not sure that it would be regarded as dance, but Chris remained unmoved. He agreed it was pure melodrama, but absolutely typical of the period from which it came. They needed, he said, something like that to establish the character of the piece. But as they developed the opening sequence, Chris says:

'We used to come against a brick wall. We could spend a whole day on it and not create a single step. The only way we were making any progress was that we were eliminating what was not going to work. We experienced a degree of frustration that we had not known before and I was coming near to the dangerous conclusion that we could improve no further, that we could do no better than we had done in previous years. Betty was away at the time so we could get no help from her, but we slogged away and when she got back to Oberstdorf we'd got through it. When we discovered how delighted she was with it, the cloud lifted. She would just come and stand with

A sequence from the haunting blues OSP of the 1981/2 season; it elicited the then record of six 6.0s (from seven judges), to be surpassed by seven 6.0s (from nine judges) in the world championships of 1983 at Helsinki (top left *Ice & Roller Skate Magazine*, remainder *All-Sport Photographic*)

us in the small rink, putting the music on for us and saying very little. She'd just save us the trouble of going to wind it back, because she obviously knows when we want to stop and start again. When she's there with us everything's fine, but we get irritable if anyone else is about. **9**

For every frustration in creating a new programme there is compensating exhilaration. True, they would sometimes get nothing from a whole day on the ice. But the next day, a glimmer will show through and that in turn would lead on to something else and then they would be in full flow. It is rather like a jigsaw puzzle, where a key piece would slot into place and open the way for many more, before a new hiatus awaits the next key piece. Michael Stylianos went out to Oberstdorf for nearly a week at this time, with less effect than before. They discovered that he was a valuable ally in perfecting a dance but not in creating it on the ice in the first instance. He was, though, a good influence for Jayne, since he could get her to move in a way that, Betty Callaway says, was beyond her own powers of persuasion. The only mistake with *Mack and Mabel* was that they had got the music settled without a single idea what to do with it. Jayne:

6We always say you need the music first but, having heard the music, you need to go and play around on the ice without music but with the theme in mind. We had not done much of that preparation. Generally we were trying to move step by step with every note. Some days we realised this mistake and we would decide to forget the music and just start messing around. Like those scissors steps in the *Mack and Mabel* train sequence. That came from just fooling around. One day we had a light-hearted spin in the small rink in front of the mirror and those scissors steps suddenly came from nowhere. We were laughing because we couldn't synchronise our steps and kept stumbling. When we looked at what we were doing from the side in the mirror we realised it looked quite interesting. The piece of music really lent itself to that sort of treatment. We quarrelled quite a bit putting that programme together and got depressed at times when nothing would come, but I remember having a lot of fun, too, once we'd got it settled and begun to skate out. **9**

But it was another leap into the unknown and they wanted some reassurance that *Mack and Mabel*, so different in concept from any previous free dance, would be acceptable. The rules lay down that no more than three changes of rhythm would be allowed, but they had lifted four minutes virtually intact from the overture to the show, so there was not one artificial transition. The piece flowed and any changes of tempo were introduced by the music itself. It was revolutionary and, as it turned out, revelational.

When they got back to Nottingham at the end of July they arranged for two judges living in Birmingham, Roy Mason and Mary Parry, to come up to Nottingham and pass an opinion. Chris and Jayne wore matching outfits rather than informal practice gear to achieve a better effect, and fully expected to have to break off during the programme since they had only just got to the point of running through it unbroken. In fact they skated it without a hiccup and the semi-official verdict was simple. Don't change a step, their consultants said, don't change a single note. 'Mary,' Jayne reports, 'was jumping up and down in her excitement.'

Then they did their OSP, to what Chris describes as an ecstatic audience of two. Betty was not there on that occasion. Roy Mason and Mary Parry expressed one small doubt, about a loop in the blues. That year the ISU had ruled against 'regressions' because some skaters were taking too much time on the ice, taking liberties with the idea of three circuits of OSP. The judges suggested they might try their luck with it, as it was a tiny loop on a single edge, but it was to incur the wrath of Lawrence Demmy at the St Ivel a month or two later.

The other important activity of the summer was the design of costumes to match the mood of the two moments, the sombre blues and the jauntily romantic free. Bobby Thompson answered the first demand, Courtney Jones the second. Thompson created a plain black blouse-type outfit for Chris, almost devoid of embellishment, that was exactly in tune with their OSP. For Jayne he produced a pretty, dark little number, low-cut behind because, he declares, 'Jayne has a perfect back', and with an odd ribbon or two streaming from the shoulders. Jones came up with gold costumes for *Mack and Mabel*, because 'with his fair hair Chris needs gold'. Jayne had another exceptionally pretty dress with feathery skirt, Chris a suit with button-front jacket. Together, they made a riveting spectacle.

Training that August was difficult at Nottingham, with the children on holiday, and they could skate only late at night to any real purpose. Then, unexpectedly, they got the chance of a couple of weeks away. They were invited to St Gervais for exhibitions—they were in heavy demand now as world champions—and were able to go on to Oberstdorf for a week. They took the wraps off their new programmes at the St Ivel at Richmond that September and immediately proved that their victories in the Europeans and worlds the previous winter had been no fluke. That removed another doubt.

Even Betty Callaway, who knew them better than anyone else, had been 'a little concerned that they had got to the top so quickly and would have to maintain it for so long before the Olympics came round again in 1984.'

For Eileen Anderson, the team leader, Innsbruck 1981 had been 'a shock pure and simple. I was frightened they would have to carry so much pressure before the Winter Games.' St Ivel 1981 put all minds at rest. If the gold were to elude them at Sarajevo in 1984, it would not be for any want of enduring quality. 'I could see them grow day by day,' Betty Callaway says, 'and by the time the worlds were behind us that 1981–2 winter I realised they were capable of heights I hadn't even dreamed of'. Even more gratifying, perhaps, was the way they were carrying themselves. 'If anything,' Betty adds,' they became so determined to be good champions that they were almost humbled by it really.'

The OSP almost caused a diplomatic incident, since the Russians were seen filming it at Richmond for video reproduction. In fact, they seemed to point their camera at Chris and Jayne every time they set foot on the ice. Betty was little concerned about the compulsories or the free dance, which were outside the range of sporting espionage—the former because of strict control of every step by the ISU, the latter because of its personal character. 'The Russians are strong in free dancing, anyway, with their own individuality,' she says, 'but a thing like the blues was not part of their culture, so they would be looking around for ideas. They might not have lifted anything specific, but an idea of what the blues really was. It was more a breach of etiquette than anything else. I wouldn't have dreamed of filming any of their couples in London, never mind Moscow.' Jayne thought the attention they got from the Russians was flattering.

Chris saw it differently: 'Nobody in his right mind would try to copy you but it was like seeing a new car before it had been presented. Your competitors would be anxious to know what was new about it, try to pick it apart. It was early in the season, with four months to go before the European championships and another month before the worlds. They had time to study your stuff and maybe if there were any grounds for criticism they could find it.'

'Having said that,' Jayne adds, 'the Russians were some of the first people to come up and congratulate us. Even in practice, the trainers of the other couples were saying they really liked what we

Jayne surrenders to the mood of the moment and to her masterful partner in one of the many evocative passages from the rumba (*All-Sport Photographic*)

were doing, thought the choreography was so good. So we should not hammer them at all. What they did, they didn't do in a bad way, but we wouldn't have done it in Moscow, for example. I can't really see why they did it, unless they wanted a way of simply showing the people on their committee what was happening elsewhere. We would rather not know what other people are doing. We go our own way, and if someone else can come up with something better that's up to them.'

St Ivel was a glittering triumph—not in terms of position, since the principal opposition came from two other British couples, but of performance. Chris and Jayne received one 6.0 for their OSP, another milestone, and three 6.0s for the free from the judges of Canada, Austria and the Soviet Union. Even when allowance is made for the fact that the Russian couple in the St Ivel lay fifth and therefore allowed their judge total freedom of movement without possible charges of domestic disloyalty, his six was an eye-opener. The news sped round the skating world and so prepared everyone for the triumphs ahead.

The OSP had not met with universal approval. In spite of those high marks, or rather because of them, Lawrence Demmy was critical of the judges for allowing the loop to go unpunished. Betty was told that innocent little loop had to go. In the light of what was to happen it can hardly have been vital to the performance.

The next hurdle was the British championship in November, but before then they were summoned to Buckingham Palace to be decorated with the MBE. They had been sounded out in advance, as is the way with the honours lists, and heard for certain on 13 June, the Queen's birthday, by way of a call from a radio reporter. They had known of the possibility for three months but tried to thrust it to the back of their minds in case there should be a hitch.

It was a tantalising period, wondering if somebody might have thrown a spanner in the works. They were at Oberstdorf when the word came through and felt a little cheated. An MBE does not exactly set the Rhine on fire, so there was nobody except Betty with whom they could share their excitement. It was the one occasion when they would have wished that their wise counsellor could have dropped her normal air of serene composure. It should have been a moment for dancing in the streets.

When the day came in October to see the Queen, they arranged to stay at the home of a friend in Richmond, Margaret Jones, a convenient London *pied-à-terre* only five minutes from the rink. They had to dress up for the occasion, as Jayne reports: 'That was the funniest thing. My outfit cost a fortune. Chris went to hire a morning suit in Nottingham and they let him have it for nothing

The conventional pose outside Buckingham Palace after receiving their MBEs from the Queen in October 1981 (*Press Association*)

when they discovered what it was for. They recognised him, of course, and had heard about the MBE. They even altered the suit here and there, something they would not do in the ordinary course of events. He had to make do with a felt topper, poor lad, because they hadn't a silk one in stock at the time.' They assume husband and wife stereotypes in telling what happened on the day:

❛J: After we'd all been to Mrs Jones's for dinner the night before, including our parents, we had to be up early next morning. Can you imagine the state he's in, with his obsession for punctuality? We had to be there by eleven, so we had to leave at eight! And we sat along the Mall for hours.

C: We did not. We were there for about half an hour with the rest of the cars that were there before us. Jayne would have gone there in the rush hour and arrived two hours late.

J: And listen to this. I dropped the hat! We were just getting in the car and away it went.

C: If Jayne's wearing clean clothes and she's got to do anything like that she's sure to get it dirty. She's just a baby.

J: It had got little splashes on it. His mum had some talcum powder and we were putting talc on the hat to make it dry. My heart dropped. I'd spent a bomb on the outfit and now this. I wouldn't dare tell Chris how much it cost, otherwise he'd murder me.

C: I wouldn't mind so much if only you looked after things.

J: But here's the best part. Just before we left he said he hadn't got his ticket, he'd left it in Nottingham.

C: I knew she'd tell you that.

J: He said we needn't worry, because they'd know what we looked like. We wouldn't need it. Well, when we got to the gate the first thing the policeman said was: 'Have you got your invitations?' Chris said: 'Er, well, we've got two here and there's two there' and was trying to wriggle round it. I said straight out: 'He's forgotten his.' I mean, if you try to tell fibs they never work. Pointless him saying all those stupid things.

C: I'd thought it was just a card telling you the time and everything.

J: We had to park in a certain place. A dog came and went in the boot and when he re-emerged without a smoking bomb in his mouth, we were allowed in. There was a man in funny dress, an usher I suppose, and there were some gawkers.

C: Ghurkas, I think you mean.

J: Then there were these men on the stairs, who looked like statues wearing a sort of armour, on guard.

C: Was that what they were there for?

J: Well, I shouldn't imagine they'll stand there all day if nothing's happening, nobody coming. Would you? We did all this thing and I thought we'd get a cup of coffee or something. But we didn't get anything.

C: Not a damned thing.

J: And we'd spent all that money! At least I had.

C: And you don't need half of it anyway. You leave your hat and gloves in the cloakroom. We were led into a huge hall, roped off for CBEs, OBEs, MBEs, etc. There was another room for the knights.

J: They didn't get coffee, either.

C: I think she expected a woman to come round with a trolley, like they do in works canteens. We were about the youngest there and a few people recognised us, army chaps I think. We were given a little demo on how to walk. All the others were going up individually, but we were to go up together, so we had to rehearse. The worst of it was..

J: ...they never told us where the bathroom was! I bet everybody would have gone if only they'd known where it was.

C: Maybe that's why everybody sat cross-legged. We were then led from this room into another section and you just have to follow the red carpet. The Queen is in the middle bit. All the audience is there and they've got one of the bands playing quietly in the background. They're all sitting there waiting for us to arrive. They get the whole show. And you see only the bit that you are in, unless you're at the beginning, in which case you can go back and watch the rest. You walk up and bow, or curtsey, and call the Queen Ma'am.

J: We'd been announced as Miss Jayne Torvill and Mr Christopher Dean, but nobody clapped or anything. The Queen said she was glad the title had come back to Britain after twelve years. She seemed to know all about it. She asked how long we planned to carry on and seemed pleased to know that we'd go on to the next Olympics. You've already got a pin on you and she just hooks the medal on to it.

C: You walk out and they give you the book with all the other bits. It was marvellous for the first ten minutes, but then it got boring. You've been there for two hours without even a cup of coffee. We finally plucked up courage and asked where the loo was.

J: We've made a bit of a joke about it here, but it was quite a thrill. I'd go again tomorrow if they asked me. Afterwards we had a meal in the hotel, drove back to Nottingham and were on the rink by eleven o'clock that same night. The British was drawing near and we'd already given up one night. Missing another would have been unthinkable. **9**

The British championship of 1981 was a special occasion, since Chris and Jayne were competing in their own city for the first time since becoming world champions. They were coming home to claim their kingdom. By now the country had come to regard them as their own and bask in the reflected glory and they responded magnificently. Whereas some might have faltered under the burden of expectancy, they were inspired to even greater heights. Chris draws some satisfaction from their ability to cope with such pressure:

❝You can easily tell when we are under pressure because we go so quiet, specially me. I don't much like having people around whom I know. I would much rather be isolated. If we should happen to chance on somebody we know at such a time, I'm apt to walk away and cause Jayne embarrassment. It's not that I want to be rude, but I'm in no mood for conversation at such a time and am better out of the way. But what happens on the ice is what matters and I think we discovered something important at Nottingham that night. We could take the pressure. That's one thing that only comes from the experience. Until you're subjected to it you have no way of knowing how it will affect you. We found that, if anything, we perform better under pressure. Nottingham, in front of our own people, was much more of a test than Hartford had been. ❞

Nottingham was also punishing, because there were only six entries and the whole of the championship was completed in one evening. It meant that the skaters had to raise themselves five times within a few hours, three times for the compulsories and once each for the OSP and free. Chris, particularly, was tired going into the free, but overcame it to such purpose that they knocked the judging panel for six, or rather nine astonishing 6.0s. They were given two 6.0s for technical merit in the free and seven (out of nine) for artistic impression. The two who stood aloof on the second mark were the two former world champions on the panel, Lawrence Demmy and Courtney Jones.

The prize capture at Nottingham was Pamela Davis, who had been on record as saying that she had never given a six nor ever would. Now she gave not one but two. Why did she surrender so totally? '1. They were technically brilliant. 2. They have a beautiful soft knee with a rise and fall which is the essence of dance. 3. They have softness and quietness on turns of a high quality, with no scrapes or scratches. 4. The carriage was immaculately well held, without looking stiff and tight, relaxed without being limp. 5. The timing was flawless. 6. Their musical conception was superb, each dance interpreted that little bit differently from everyone else. 7. A rapport as deep as they achieved is so rare. 8. They were lost in the music and came over as one. And, if that were not enough, they've got a magic personality on the ice. I can watch *Mack and Mabel*, and their 'Summertime' for that matter, for ever and never be bored. That's not so much rare as unprecedented in my experience.'

Lawrence Demmy was still not absolutely satisfied with their OSP, in spite of the removal of the offending loop. He gave them only 5.6 and 5.7. That was forgotten, however, an hour or so later when the audience sprang to their feet as one to acclaim *Mack and Mabel* in a pandemonium of applause that went on and on, to be repeated when the marks were displayed. It was a memorable moment, for Nottingham was now able to express a city's pride at what had happened the season before, to pay tribute not only to four minutes of *Mack and Mabel* magic, but also to their Innsbruck and Hartford triumphs. 'Everybody we spoke to afterwards,' Chris says, 'seemed to be as high as we were.'

They did not sleep that night, with the cheers still ringing in their ears, and the next morning they made their usual pilgrimage to present flowers to Betty in her hotel, a characteristically modest little establishment away from the city centre. It was a routine gesture of thanks, but more heartfelt than at any time before. A week or so later they were back at the rink for a unique occasion, the first gold star test ever taken by ice dancers. A number of figure skaters have done so on the strength of four minutes of free skating (five minutes for a man, now four and a half), but Chris and Jayne had to perform the whole of their repertoire of that season, three compulsories, the OSP and free, together with the three compulsories of the previous season, all within the space of forty minutes, as it turned out. It was a harrowing experience, as Jayne reports:

❦We did not skate well, not by our standards. I felt so stiff and nervous, and normally I'm not a bit like that. It was such a surprise to Chris that it made him jittery, and that's not like him. Normally with a test you get four or five people watching, almost by accident, but here there was a crowd of nearly 1,000 paying 50p each to charity plus five judges, the TV and the press. It was weird, uncanny, as if we were suspended in a glass jar for examination. What made it worse was the fact that we'd have felt daft if we'd failed, but on the other hand we didn't want it to be given to us if we weren't good enough.

Well, fortunately we were good enough, though we had to do the rumba twice, because the timing wasn't quite right. That was one of the three dances from the previous year and I suppose we tended to skip it during our run-up to the British championship. We only did the gold star to add to our portfolio. With the other tests you get a certificate and you can buy a medal if you wish. We've not bought one, but we might have considered the gold star because of its uniqueness. In fact, the NSA had two made specially for us. **9**

They proposed to take a rare holiday now, having no cause to tamper with the OSP or free, but it was squeezed at both ends and came down eventually to seven days, in Miami Beach. They were delayed going out by the British figure skating championships, where they were to give exhibitions, and the Skaters' Ball in London, where they were honoured guests. At the other end, they had to cut short their holiday in order to appear at the Sports Writers' Association dinner to celebrate their selection as the Team of the Year.

Jayne was also voted the Sportswoman of the Year, a separate distinction that might have caused domestic strife, but Chris took it in good part. He could not resist some good-natured ribbing, but that was as far as it went. As Jayne readily admitted, the competition among the men was so much stronger with people like Sebastian Coe around. She is not sure she would have reacted so generously if Chris had got the men's award and she nothing. So it was that she had to open the evening's dancing, officially, with Coe, but he ducked it, so she had to force a cringing Chris on to the floor. Now, Chris gets about 2.4 for technical merit for ballroom dancing and not much more for artistic impression, but at least he made the effort. Then Jayne left him to insist on Seb Coe doing his duty. She was by now highly skilled in leading people a dance.

Lyons roar of approval

With Christmas 1981 and a well-received exhibition appearance in Zurich behind them, Chris and Jayne were back in Oberstdorf preparing for the European championships in Lyons. Michael Stylianos came out for a while to better purpose this time since the steps had been set and he could concentrate on body, arm and leg positions. For Chris the *Mack and Mabel* programme was physically taxing, with several unusual lifts, in one of which he hoists Jayne with his hands under her shoulder blades in the back. It is followed by a twist that brings them face to face, a novel movement explained by Chris as springing from the original lift:

❢Whenever you think of a different move, you have then to consider how the hell you're going to get out of it. The difference between our branch of the sport and pair skating is that in between they've got a lot of forward running and backward crossovers –plain stuff—so you can get your energy back. You do it every day when you skate, so it's an easy recuperation point, whereas in ice dance every step you make is, or should be, trying to be creative, trying to do something. You haven't got time to take a deep breath. And Jayne's not as small as people think, 5ft zero certainly but weighing $7\frac{1}{2}$ stone. We don't consciously think we can't afford to have a breathing space, but the way we construct a programme we don't want to do anything plain if we can put in something interesting. If something looks plain, it's wrong.　　　　　❜

Chris now suffered yet another eve-of-championship sickness. Because of an early flight from Munich to Lyons they stopped overnight at a friend's house in Munich. After a meal out Chris was ill all night and he felt as if Moiseyeva's revenge was upon him. For twenty-four hours he took in nothing more than black tea and felt drained when the time came for competition, unusually a day earlier on the Tuesday at Lyons because there were only nine entries for the pairs and the first day's programme had to be strengthened. They had felt so fit and strong before leaving Oberstdorf and its invigorating 843 metres (2,750 feet) above sea level, but fortunately his recovery was rapid because he was in peak physical condition. It did little for his health or his peace of mind when, on arrival at Lyons, they had to share a taxi for forty minutes with a coughing, sneezing, sniffing driver who puffed acrid cigarette smoke, offensive to them at the best of times, in a confined atmosphere with all windows closed. It was a cold, wet, dark morning and the hotel at the top of a business complex gave no facility for opening a window nor any help with the luggage. A flow of vitamin C tablets and fresh fruit aided the recovery.

When the competition started Chris and Jayne were glad of the Tuesday start: because they were skating with the pairs, they had a sizeable audience—an unusual luxury for the compulsories. Once they got started they found they were in such good form that they enjoyed themselves, with Chris rapidly regathering his powers. They felt relaxed, their confidence buttressed by the fact that the British and St Ivel had convinced them that they had something special to offer. They found they were the target of close scrutiny by the other skaters and curiosity of the non-specialists, a sure sign that they were people who mattered. When the Russians, their principal challengers, were around the defending champions would be inclined to put on more of a show, apply some psychological pressure. Chris and Jayne paid little attention to their competitors, not in any Olympian or arrogant spirit of detachment, but simply because they preferred not to know what other people were up to.

They landed an early blow when the championship started, with a silky-smooth blues—the prescribed pattern blues, not the one they had devised for the OSP. They were all elegance and easy grace and received marks up to 5.8, generous for a compulsory. But an early start in the blues coupled with a late start in the next dance, the yankee polka, placed an absurdly long interval of four hours between the two. There was even time for them to go back to their hotel and have a bite to eat, a novel experience during competition.

The ruts had bitten deep before they came to do their polka, but even so they performed well, 'better than in the worlds a month later,' Chris later confessed. The ruts are less of a problem with the yankee polka, since it is a new dance and people have different approaches to it. The pattern varies. The Viennese waltz 'is one that separates the sheep from the goats', according to Chris:

6It's a difficult dance because you stay in the same hold all the time and everything is done face to face, with the lady virtually doing mirror steps to the man. Everything has to match up, all the edges have to be pretty much the same to be able to go in the same direction. There are deep edges as well, so for that dance out of all dances you have to have great unison. If you don't have a good basic technique you can forget about it. The thing is you can't dress it up, because it's in the waltz hold position. You can't hide it with fancy movements or anything like that. 9

They had worked on the Viennese waltz and were rewarded with marks ranging as high as 5.9 and no lower than 5.7. They had won the three prescribed pattern dances by an overwhelming margin, placed first by every judge for every dance except for a couple of tied marks—by the Italian judge for the blues and the Russian judge for the yankee polka. In each case their rivals were Bestemianova and Bukin, who were completing the eclipse of their illustrious compatriots, Moiseyeva and Minenkov.

When the couples took the ice for the OSP warm-up Chris and Jayne immediately stamped their mark on the proceedings. Whereas the others skated as couples, first tracing flowing figures of eight side by side over the whole of the area and later rehearsing certain key passages from their routine, the British couple took off in different directions from the start and skated separately, as though completely oblivious to each other's presence. They had done this all season at home, but it was an eye-opener in an international championship. Chris explains:

‘We came to realise there were many good reasons for warming up separately and none for continuing with the usual practice. In the first place, it was false. We never do that in normal training. Our practice is to spend the first few minutes skating around on our own, to get the feel of the ice before we come together. Why abandon that idea on the comparatively few occasions when we warm up before a live audience at a major competition? If it is right to do it one way for most of the time, how can it be right to do it another way only on the big occasion? Then again, it is quite hairy out there with five or six couples whipping around, either engrossed in their little rehearsals which make them a danger to other people as well as themselves or, which is mostly the case, they have half an eye on what other people are doing and therefore cannot skate with full attention.

An accident was the last thing we wanted at that stage after the months of work we'd put into our training. If by now you haven't got the programme completely mastered, one more try will not make any difference. But if you make a boob it's going to do nothing for your morale. Also we didn't want to show anything before the music came on. The music is all part of what you're doing and it will look quite different without the music. It might create the wrong impression. Little bits of ‘Summertime’ or *Mack and Mabel* without the music wouldn't have made any sense. We felt, at the same time, that we were hiding our hands, from the audience that is. The judges will have seen us in practice of course, if not at a previous competition.

If you have any really special highlights, as we like to think we always have, you will achieve the maximum impact with the audience if you spring them on them when it's for real. It seemed a more professional attitude. After all, you don't see actors coming on the stage before the play begins for a bit of rehearsal. We weren't conscious of creating a precedent but a lot of other people mentioned it to us afterwards, including some skaters. **'**

It was a departure that showed, once again, that original minds were at work. No announcements are made at the time of warm-up and the rink is alive with murmurings as the spectators discuss the couples now parading before them and try to identify them. Yes, Irina Moiseyeva has the classical good looks; Natalya Bestemianova is the auburn-haired beauty with the tall partner; the bouncy little number is the English girl, Karen Barber, with her smiling companion, Nicky Slater.

Who then are the couple in black, floating around on their own? Perhaps they've had a row. Their identity, less obvious then than now, will percolate through in time. Christopher Dean and Jayne Torvill were distinctive from the rest. It might have been seen as a gimmick, but, as Chris has explained, there were reasons for their routine.

Unknown to the audience they had also struck out in a different direction during practice. At every session they had given the whole works, whether set dances, OSP or free. One circuit of the OSP was not good enough for them: they skated all three with their lead-in and finishing flourish. In the free dance practice, they had taken *Mack and Mabel* right through the whole range of their experiences in the silent movie era, whereas other couples would pick up only certain sections of their programme.

It was irritating to any spectators who might be there at the time and certainly to judges who were trying to get a sneak preview. Pamela Davis, one of the senior British judges, says: 'When skaters do their full programme it's bound to make a good impression. There's nothing more annoying than to see a couple break off in practice.' Again Chris and Jayne were following their normal routine. Except when they are making up a programme or perfecting small passages, it is their habit to run through it from start to finish. Chris again:

'Every time you do the programme in full you're adding to your store of experience and self-confidence. The more you can drill yourself into automatic mastery on the ice, the more you can give to presentation when the big moment comes. You can, in other words, expand in other directions without the fear that something might go technically wrong. I'm not saying you can insure yourself totally against error—remember our OSP at Dortmund in 1980?—but if you're confident about the technical side you can give more attention to putting it across. It also builds up your physical condition when you do that time after time along with a lot of other activity, on the ice and on the floor.

In practice we sometimes do our free dance twice in succession, with an interval in between for only as long as it takes to rewind the tape. I think other skaters would be wary of doing a full run-through as championship practice, either because they would fear making a mistake in the presence perhaps of some of the judges, or because they are not as fit as they should be. Every time you do a full run-through you're giving a performance and generally people only want to do that on the night. They want to be 'up' for it on one occasion and pull it off then, which I can understand. But we like to get into a position when we can do it any time we want and then add a special spark when the chips are down.

We used to find that doing the full thing became an effort if we spent a whole week just doing sections. However good or impressive they were, at the back of your mind you're wondering 'God, what's going to happen when we do the whole thing?' Again, I think we gained a tactical advantage at Lyons, and later Copenhagen. Although there were good reasons for the change, we were aware at the same time of putting psychological pressure on the others, because people commented on it. They'd say 'you must be fit, you must be confident'. Skaters who had to follow us at practice wondered if they ought to follow suit, or were urged by their trainer to do so. From what people said to us we realised that we were making other skaters feel that slight bit inferior. That was never our intention, but we're not apologising!   **9**

Their view of the Lyons OSP is mixed. That it was a raging success there could be no doubt, whether measured in audience reaction or judges' evaluation. The French rise to ice dance, although their national record is not outstanding. They hold a competition confined entirely to dance at Morzine, south of Geneva every year.

It may be for that reason that Chris and Jayne were more concerned to seek precision and technical perfection than to pour all their emotion into the piece. Their own full satisfaction would follow at Copenhagen, but for the moment they achieved their objective so far as everyone else in the stadium was concerned. The crowd was eager to applaud every highlight, so much so that the third circuit was performed to a volley of unbroken applause. The judges responded in the same elated vein with three pairs of 5.9 for composition and 6.0 for presentation. The British couple had never before exceeded 5.8 for an OSP. Chris tries to explain his lukewarm reaction some months later:

❢We skated it well, but I felt we skated it carefully. I think we felt as if they were expecting a lot from it and I didn't think we lost ourselves in it as we did later at Copenhagen. Can't say what it was. I wouldn't say we skated it less well than at Copenhagen, but it came over differently. It's just what we felt inside. You might think that should have come out on the ice, but when you become proficient at what you're doing, more 'professional' if you like, you can still go on and give a performance even if you think that a dance doesn't feel quite right. ❢

Is all this a trick of hindsight, in the knowledge of what they were to do with 'Summertime' at Copenhagen? Everything points that way, from the audience, from the judges and from fellow competitors. Natalya Bestemianova, their nearest challenger at the side of Andrei Bukin, went out of her way to congratulate them, together with the couple's trainer, Tatiana Tarasova. Another witness in favour of Lyons is Joan Wallis, the team leader. She had seen the OSP before at the British, but as the referee at Nottingham she had not been able to take it in fully. Now she saw it as a bystander and, she says, 'the full emotion hit me. There were strong men standing round me with tears running down their faces. It was unbelievable.'

Pamela Davis regarded 'Summertime' as 'beautifully skated, exactly right for that music. Not all that difficult, perhaps, by their standards, but difficult enough and with attractive highlights to grip the public and the judges.' I can add that a former German ice dancer was almost in a trance. 'It was like a dream,' she told me, and pinched her arm to indicate, where her English failed her, that it had made her flesh tingle.

After the OSP the ice dancers, unusually, had a day's break because of the decline in pair skating. They spent the spare day pottering about, mostly on their own. In earlier times they would have mixed more with the other skaters, but now they felt they had so much on their minds that they preferred to relax independently. There was shopping, television and some practice so far as that was allowable. They were at the rink in the evening for the men's final, dramatically and boisterously interrupted by an invasion of the ice by supporters of Poland's Solidarity trade union.

On the following evening Wendy Sessions expressed the hope that the ice dance final would also be disrupted. Jayne and Karen Barber pleaded with Wendy to behave, not to spread herself over the dressing-room floor after she had skated, as was often her abandoned way. Would she please go away and hide? In fact, she contented herself with a somersault by way of relief from tension. In the men's dressing-room Chris was motivating himself and coming to terms with the loss of his dressing-room which had been taken over for doping control. He had found another corner in the second dressing-room early enough in the week to be relatively undisturbed.

Chris and Jayne were drawn to skate last, after Bestemianova and Bukin. The relative position of the two couples mirrored that between the British couple and Moiseyeva and Minenkov the previous year. Britain had won the compulsories, including the OSP conclusively, but a victory for Bestemianova and Bukin in the free would have given them the gold medal on the tie-break system. Chris and Jayne hovered silently at the back while the Russian couple skated—without hearing the spectators' applause, without seeing the judges' marks and certainly without speaking to anyone. Bestemianova and Bukin lean heavily on her personality and technical wizardry. She has a strong presence and a full repertoire of tricks, but perhaps she comes on a little too strong and tends to overshadow her partner. Apart from one slow passage, the programme was all rather frenetic and breathless—over-choreographed in most places, according to Bobby Thompson, and under-choreographed in others. They were well marked, however, as Chris and Jayne glided around in one corner of the rink waiting to be called, lost in their own little world. The Russians had six marks of 5.9 and nothing below a 5.7 from the Austrian judge, Rudolf Zorn. Mary Parry, of Britain, gave them two 5.8s.

The champions sensed a special atmosphere that night at Lyons. The French love of ice dance had lifted the temperature as the evening wore on and as Torvill and Dean came to close the proceedings they felt the spectators were on the edge of their seats, ready for a pulsating climax. They were not disappointed. Yet the British couple, 'not entirely robots' Chris points out, were assailed by a number of small doubts. To begin with, there had been problems with the music during the week. The speeds of different machines vary and after practising with their own tapes they now skated to a master tape on which their music had been re-recorded.

That fear proved unfounded, as was another concerning a lift half a minute into the programme. For this, Jayne throws herself on to Chris's hip, whence he twirls her round horizontally before putting her back on the ice. It had not gone smoothly in some practices and it was the most perilous moment of the whole performance. That,

Jayne swinging round Chris before striking their final dramatic pose of *Mack and Mabel* in 1982 (*Ice & Roller Skate Magazine*)

too, was safely negotiated and another, more mysteriously, occupied their mind. At some point in practice an aberration on Jayne's part had caused Chris to ask plaintively: 'What are you doing, Jayne?' and look at his partner, according to her 'as if I'd gone absolutely mad'. Chris maintains that he is the constant factor in the partnership and Jayne the one 'who's always changing things, just to vary the training, I reckon.' Whatever it was, it did not recur at Lyons when it mattered and at long last they were through to the change of tempo, signalled by a backward leap by Jayne, like a reckless salmon on to a welcoming knee.

With that breathtaking move out of the way, the road was clear for *Mack and Mabel* to declare their love and Chris and Jayne their pre-eminence. The excitement grew with each new *coup de théâtre*, until they came to the train sequence that lit up the whole performance. They could hardly hear the music from then on because of the swelling ovation. Betty, serene and composed as ever, greeted them with a smile, little more, and when the marks came up Chris feinted behind his glowing partner's back as an expression of mock disbelief. They got three 6.0s for the first mark (technical merit) and eight out of nine for the second (artistic impression). Eleven 6.0s established a record for international championships, and their fourteen for the whole event—taking into account the three for the OSP—was another highwater mark.

Since there was—then—no precedent for fourteen 6.0s in any form of ice skating, it is worth giving the Lyons marks in full:

	1	2	3	4	5	6	7	8	9
COMPULSORY DANCES									
Blues	5.7	5.7	5.6	5.5	5.8	5.7	5.5	5.8	5.7
Yankee Polka	5.8	5.7	5.7	5.8	5.9	5.6	5.7	5.9	5.8
Viennese Waltz	5.9	5.7	5.7	5.8	5.8	5.7	5.7	5.7	5.7
ORIGINAL SET PATTERN DANCE									
Composition	5.9	5.7	5.8	5.7	5.9	5.8	5.9	5.8	5.8
Presentation	6.0	5.9	5.9	5.8	6.0	5.8	6.0	5.9	5.8
INITIAL ROUND									
Total points	29.3	28.7	28.7	28.6	29.4	28.6	28.8	29.1	28.8
Placing	1	1	1	1	1	1	1	1	1
FREE DANCE									
Technical merit	5.9	5.9	5.9	6.0	6.0	5.9	6.0	5.9	5.9
Artistic impression	6.0	6.0	6.0	6.0	6.0	5.9	6.0	6.0	6.0
Total points	11.9	11.9	11.9	12.0	12.0	11.8	12.0	11.9	11.9
Placing	1	1	1	1	1	1	1	1	1

Judges: 1 Miss Mary Parry (GB)
2 Mrs Marina Greminger (Switzerland)
3 Milan Duchon (Czechoslovakia)
4 Vinicio Toncelli (Italy)
5 Daniel de Paix (France)
6 Igor Kabanov (USSR)
7 Rudolf Zorn (Austria)
8 Istvan Sugar (Hungary)
9 Heinz Mullenbach (W Germany)

Chris and Jayne were 'absolutely stunned by the marks'. They knew they had skated well and they knew, with no skaters to follow, the judges could afford to be generous if they felt so disposed, but they had no idea that they would surrender so comprehensively. The *Sunday Times*, seeking an original angle on the new superstars, had the interesting idea of diverting their dance critic, David Dougill, to the ice and thereby produced the following penetrating appreciation:

❝It was a punchy and dramatic opening—Dean fast in pursuit, Torvill spurning him—which in a few seconds established characters and a 'situation' to hold the taut, dazzling display together. An ingenious choice of music, self-contained—not 'cobbled together'—carefree and rag-timey, and lyrical for the central *adage*, allowed seamless, logical transitions in tempo and mood, and admirable fluency, precision and speed in the steps, spiced with unpredictable effects. Somehow, when at full tilt forward, Torvill twice circumnavigated Dean in the twinkling of an eye. Neat and delightful were her series of *piqué* sideways steps while supported across his back. Nothing obviously showy; never a trick because 'that's expected on the ice'; never an ugly 'in-between' position. More than once I was reminded of the choreographer Kenneth MacMillan's deft, daredevil *pas de deux* in ballet. I loved the snatched embrace—a moment of tenderness—and the witty suggestion of a train journey, perfectly fitting the music, abruptly ended in a superb change of direction, and leading to a fine unforced finish. A performance of showbiz dash and technical wizardry, controlled by an unusual sensitivity.   ❞

Unfortunately Lyons ended as it had begun, on a low note. Having sat through nearly four hours of exhibitions on the Sunday afternoon, Chris and Jayne were at the centre of a fiasco when, skating last, they had to suffer a wholesale muddle on the part of the man in charge of the music. It was an unfortunate farewell. Jayne carried home a Lyons lion, too big to join her three 'paddy bears' in her travelling entourage.

They were not sorry to see the back of Lyons, despite their block-busting success, but Nottingham was another trial, for they were now so well-known. They hardly set foot outside their homes except to go to the rink late at night and they became so sickened of the straitjacket that they returned to Oberstdorf earlier than they had intended to prepare for Copenhagen. They trained hard between Lyons and Copenhagen. Chris:

❝You've had a high and come down from it with a few days at home. It's a good thing really that you come down. You have to tune up again like a motor car. You don't expect it to be the same for the next race without having to do anything with it. You have to rebuild it, because it's been worn down. We had two weeks at Oberstdorf

Chris and Jayne acknowledge the applause for their second European gold medal after *Mack and Mabel* at Lyons; Bestemianova and Bukin (left) were second and Moiseyeva and Minenkov third (*Ice & Roller Skate Magazine*)

A pointed question arouses different reactions during the press conference after the European championship victory in Lyons in 1982 (*Ice & Roller Skate Magazine*)

Chris, now much more at ease in the public eye, speaks on behalf of all the competitors during the prize-giving ceremony at Lyons (*Ice & Roller Skate Magazine*)

before worlds. The first was spent going through each section of the free dance. We'd do the first two sections, then the middle two sections, then the last two, and we'd build up like that. With the OSP we'd do the first sequence and the third, skipping the middle sequence. Then came Sunday and the lead-up to the worlds and we did everything every day, the free, the OSP and the three compulsory dances. We found the compulsories had gone off a little. **⁹**

They had been asked to do their free dance in Nottingham for a television crew, who seemed surprised when they refused. Jayne:

⁶ They said they were coming for an interview, but when they got there it was 'Can you do the free dance for us?' We just couldn't. For one thing, we had not skated for a while and were in no sort of shape to put anything on film. For another, it was a smaller rink, and yet another, it was a bitterly cold morning. Anyway, it's so difficult just to come back and do it again just like that. You can understand why people expect you to be able to do it, because you'd done it a few days before, but you really can't, not properly. You just lose things. You've got to do it every day to be sure of skating it properly, so we couldn't do it, not with any guarantee. We could have fumbled through, no doubt, but not to the standard that we would expect of ourselves. **⁹**

Wonderful Copenhagen

Copenhagen provided a superb rink for the world championships of 1982, the Brøndby-Hallen, but in other respects it was a dubious choice for the event. The main rink is so far out of town that on occasions the skaters would spend up to five hours a day travelling back and forth. One training rink was bigger than the competition rink, and freezing cold. The other had hard, white ice with sub-zero air temperatures. The pairing of the United States with Britain for practice was a serious mistake. It meant that two of the three most powerful nations were training together, each with three couples on the ice, whereas other groups were much less fraught with numbers and competitive tension. Beyond that, the Americans, or at least one of their couples, were unnecessarily assertive on the ice, storming around the rink regardless of life and limb, other people's as well as their own. Chris and Jayne felt particularly vulnerable, since they had much more to lose than anybody else on the rink if there had been an accident. The matter was settled without personal acrimony. Chris says:

❢We did it through team leaders. Betty made a complaint through our leader to theirs and the skaters most responsible were told to mend their ways, to recognise that when another couple was running through it was their duty to get out of the way. You would think that would be a matter of common courtesy as well as common sense, but they did not seem to see it that way. Some couples think they have an edge over others if they can thrash through and not have to stop. Maybe they thought it was a way of psyching people, frightening them into submission. This business may have originated with the Russians, who were renowned for never giving way, but we've been on exhibition practice with them and had no cause for complaint. Copenhagen had never organised an event of that stature before, so some creaking at the joints was to be expected, but I would have thought that the ISU could form a nucleus of a committee to move in and take responsibility for all championships. On the whole, though, Copenhagen wasn't too bad, better than Lyons, where the championships were kind of running themselves by the end. ❢

But there was another altercation over music. When Chris and Jayne started the free in practice on the main rink they could not hear it. They were about twenty seconds into it when they stopped to ask if they could start again with more volume. No, they could not. Could they, then, re-run it at the end of the practice, after everyone else had finished? No, they could not. They then asked if the staff would re-run the music at the end for sound testing only, during the resurfacing of the ice. No, they would not. Betty and Eileen Anderson were called in, still to no effect. The deadlock was broken only by telephone calls to and from the ISU. By their order the music was eventually replayed, but the practice was lost. Chris explains that with their melodramatic opening to *Mack and Mabel* they needed a strong start and they wanted to be sure that the volume would be right next time. There would only be two practices on the main rink so it had to be right for the second one if they were not to go into the championship cold. There were practices on the two other rinks, but different tapes were used, so that there was no guarantee of satisfaction in the Brøndby-Hallen.

With initial disagreement resolved, they were pleased to have the American champions, Blumberg and Seibert, in the same training group. It made a strong presence and everybody came to watch them. By now they had got their act together and their engine was purring beautifully. The world championship went marvellously for Chris and Jayne. They were so fit that the comparatively few opportunities for practice did not bother them at all. They spend about half the year at Oberstdorf at an altitude of 843 metres (about 2,750 feet) and bank the reserve of stamina that altitude confers. 'It builds into the system,' Jayne says. 'The first couple of days at Copenhagen we thought: "God, that was easy".' When the competition started they skated another superbly graceful compulsory blues, but a less convincing yankee polka, which later produced the following snatch of banter among the three of us:

❝J: Chris had this little fall in the warm-up.
C: She pushed me over again!
H: You say 'again'. When did it last happen?
J: Every time he falls I get the blame, because I've pushed him over.
H: All right then, how often have you pushed him over?
J: A lot of times here [Oberstdorf]!
C: And I've got the scars to prove it. But we rarely fall when we're at a competition. I think I fell because I leaned back, over-enthusiastic.
H: What did you feel about it at the time, a bit foolish?
C: Yes. It had never happened before.
J: Did you? I thought it was rather funny.
C: But you didn't do the falling.

J: No, I just looked at him…

C: …and there he was lying on the deck. **9**

Light-hearted though that may sound now, the fall had its effect. It made them realise that such a thing could happen at any time. They could not afford to be complacent. Chris passed the incident off well at the time with a polished bow to the spectators, but could not banish it from his mind. It made them, as they now confess, more tense and reserved. Even so, only the Canadian judge placed them second on the yankee polka with a mark of only 5.6. She had placed Blumberg and Seibert first with 5.7 and a second American pair, Fox and Dalley, old rivals of Chris and Jayne, level with the British couple on 5.6, not an unreasonable judgement, I dared to suggest at the time.

It was the only setback that the British couple suffered during the compulsories. The next day they danced a brilliant Viennese waltz that gained three marks of 5.9, three of 5.8 and one of 5.7, from the Czechoslovak judge. Split panels were used at Copenhagen, seven judges for the compulsories and seven more for the free. There followed an OSP so expressively tender and beautiful as to evoke the remark from an American spectator that 'you are lucky to see something like that once in a lifetime'. The British couple held the audience in the palms of their hands as they poured all their soul into 'Summertime'. Jayne was so moved herself that she found it hard to face the audience at the end 'because the whole thing was so sad. I had consciously to think to myself: "It's the end. Smile".' It was so different from Lyons, where the spectators applauded from time to time. At Copenhagen there was a cathedral hush as Chris and Jayne wove a magic spell. It was, they declared later, the best OSP they had ever performed. Jayne, attempting an evaluation, seemed lost for words:

6I can't remember it that well because I was lost in it and it went so quickly. I don't know about technically, but the presentation … I don't know how to explain. You could hear a pin drop, so deathly silent. It happened from the moment the music first started. I think a lot of people had seen it at Lyons, or heard about it, and it had gone down so well that there was an air of expectancy. They clapped as we came on and then went suddenly quiet until we finished. I still can't remember the different points in it. I can only remember the ending, the fact that people obviously liked it so much. **9**

The Canadian judge, Joyce Hisey, who might be regarded as the only one who was right the day before with the yankee polka, was surely the only one out of step with the OSP, with marks of 5.8 and 5.9. There was no other mark below 5.9 and six 6.0s in all, two of them from the Frenchwoman, Lysiane Lauret, another new record to add to the British haul. It was a performance of mutual commitment that reawakened questions about the personal relationship between Chris and Jayne. Two Canadian teachers at Copenhagen, seeing them live for the first time, echoed the thoughts of many when they declared that it was impossible for two people to skate together like that if they did not start off with a deep emotional attachment; they had been totally wrapped up in each other to the exclusion of everyone else in the stadium. It was, one said, so like prying upon lovers at a tender moment that one felt like a voyeur. A lady in the next seat, her eyes brimming, could only shake her head in disbelief.

Yet Copenhagen brought a disturbing new source of concern. For the first time they had both television channels competing for their attention and they seemed to be dogged at every turn by someone holding a camera, another a floodlight and a third a microphone. Alan Weeks, an experienced ice skating commentator, stood aside and allowed the newshounds to make their play. In the ordinary way the BBC, left alone in the field, will recognise that they ought not to intrude on skaters who were wound up to the full pitch of concentration for the occasion. With ITV also seeking a piece of the action, there were determined attempts on both sides to be first with new angles. This was legitimate journalistic activity but, however beneficial it may have been to viewers at home, it did nothing for the skaters. It was particularly unfortunate that a camera crew was waiting for them when they went out for the free. A pact between the two authorities would seem to be called for, similar to the one that left John Curry in peace during the 1976 Olympics at Innsbruck and the one agreed four years later on Robin Cousins's behalf—though he chose not to observe it when the news from home of the birth of his first nephew coincided with his unexpectedly successful first figure.

As it happened, the free was not quite the dazzling success of Lyons. They skated first this time, which ensured that the parade of sixes would not be repeated, but they may not have reached their Lyons peak. A later discussion of the free led to this interesting exchange:

C: During the warm-up my legs just went.
J: Did they? You didn't tell me, Chris.
C: Would you have wanted me to tell you: 'Eh, Jayne, my legs are killing me. I'm not going through with it'?
H: When did it happen?

John Curry, a model for Chris and Jayne in one respect: they would like to be able to say, when they finish, that they left a special mark as they feel Curry did (*All-Sport Photographic*)

C: When I'd been putting on my cat-suit in the dressing-room. I'd been bent in an awkward position and it kind of drained my legs. Didn't have the same feeling. Made my legs feel all stiff and I couldn't shake it out, couldn't loosen it off.

H: Had you ever had that before?

C: No, never. They just went stiff on me, in a sort of aching sense. I suppose it may have been nerves. During the warm-up it was as stiff as hell. We warmed up separately and I thought it would go off in a minute, but it didn't. The worst part of it was that when you're skating first, as we were in the last group, you always warm down more quickly, stop skating earlier, so for your last two to two-and-a-half minutes you are standing still, close to the barrier. It seems an eternity, like for ever. You can see the clock ticking away. And when they call the others off there are always some competitors at the other end of the rink and they had to wait for them, so you're stood there a little bit longer. They then announce your names and that's it. I was in no shape for the first lift, about half a minute into the free, but once we had got through that I felt OK. **'**

The second section of the dance was marked by a tiny error by Jayne when her ankle went over, but on the blind side of the judges so they could not have been aware of it. The final section, starting with the train, was a riot. That sequence is less simple than it looks, for the two skaters have to adjust their sliding feet on a descending scale of musical beat in perfect unison. The day before they had stumbled at that point, thus unintentionally illustrating the difficulties. With a later move Jayne whipped open Chris's jacket, causing him to wonder what she had done. Jayne was inclined to peep down to look at the damage, but Chris carried on with no apparent suggestion of concern or embarrassment. Jayne explains what happened to mar the aesthetic quality of their performance:

'When I put my arm round him my hand went inside and one of my fingers slipped between the buttons. I couldn't move my hand away. I had to keep tight hold so that I knew when I pulled my hand out it was going to pull the jacket open. If I'd tried to take my hand out and round, I'd have fallen over. That didn't appeal to me much. There was about a minute to go and everybody started clapping and cheering, so my apprehension vanished. I loved that part of it. There was a photograph in one magazine where we're just coming into the last lift and we're both smiling broadly, lifted by the crowd.

Ordinarily, we'd be a little bit tense, because it's such a hard lift, needing split-second timing. It had been a bit dodgy in practice. This

Lyudmila Pakhomova and Alexandr Gorschkov, outstanding ice-dance champions many times in the seventies, here competing in the 1976 Olympics (*Tony Duffy/All-Sport Photographic*)

time it went like a dream. That really gave me a buzz. It took for ever to get off the ice because of all the flowers. When the marks came up and they all screamed I thought there must be a 6.0, at least one. I couldn't see the marks properly because I was too busy on the ice, still collecting flowers. We never sat down that time [Chris: 'That really screwed up the TV people']. We didn't get a 6.0 for technical, that wasn't possible with four couples still to skate, and perhaps the jacket made a difference. But we got five out of seven for artistic and with no mark below 5.9 we won well. They had to wait for me to get off before they could announce the next couple. **9**

They were immediately approached by the BBC, but there was time for Chris to warn Jayne to put on her Nottingham City tracksuit top as their part of the sponsorship bargain. He was already wearing his own. The BBC had taken the rare step of postponing the nine o'clock news in order to accommodate the skating live. Alan Weeks told them he could hardly believe it himself when he was told that the news would have to take second billing. At the press conference they were bombarded with questions about their personal relationship, not surprisingly, for both their OSP and *Mack and Mabel* carried a deeper intensity of mutual commitment than is easily explained in platonic terms. Nevertheless, they produced their stock answer, that they were 'just good friends'. A reporter seeking confirmation at home that they were about to announce their engagement (so he said) received the reply from Betty Torvill, a spendid no-nonsense figure, that it would be news to her daughter as well as her.

They were now in seventh heaven. Lyons had been a marvellous experience, but there had still been another peak to climb. Now they had proved beyond any possible doubt that 1981 had been no fluke. The NSA gave a celebratory party that night, attended by many of the judges and by the reconciled factions of television. Alan Weeks is an old and trusted friend and Simon Reed, a new recruit for ITV, was so charming that Chris felt guilty for having had to say no to him on one occasion. Chris had to make his second prize-giving speech the following Sunday, an ordeal first sprung on him at Lyons as he had walked into the room. Jayne acknowledges, even in the bantering cross-talk that is typical of their private conversation, that he spoke well. It was further evidence of his receding self-consciousness and he is now so sure of himself that he never prepares a speech in advance.

They were somewhat nonplussed to be presented to the Queen of Denmark on the same day, between the exhibitions. 'Usually the people in her position are the ones who speak to you,' Chris says. 'You don't normally speak back to them. But she didn't. We shook hands and she just looked at us, smoking.' Jayne was disappointed that adhesive tape was used instead of ribbons around her victory flowers at Copenhagen, so she could not add to the collection of ribbons which she had tied to her skating bag since the first international gold medal—at Innsbruck in 1981.

The statistics stamp Chris and Jayne as unarguably the best ice dancers there have ever been, but statistics are a poor, mechanical substitute for personal appraisal. As someone once said, statistics are used as a drunken man uses lamp-posts, for support rather than illumination. We must turn to three experts, and first to Lawrence Demmy, a former world champion—indeed the first world champion along with Jean Westwood for four successive years—and chairman of the ice dance committee of the International Skating Union. Nobody could speak with greater authority—and nobody sings the praises of Christopher Dean and Jayne Torvill louder than he. They are in his opinion 'without doubt the finest ice dance couple I've ever seen and that means the best there has ever been so far as I am concerned'. He sees them as the third couple who have changed the character of the sport in recent times. First there were Lyudmila Pakhomova and her husband, Alexandr Gorschkov, in the early 1970s, and then their Russian compatriots, Irina Moiseyeva and her husband, Andrei Minenkov. He refutes, in passing, the suggestion commonly heard during the seventies that he is pro-Russian. 'I am pro-ice dance and unprejudiced in any direction.'

Pakhomova was, he thought, outstanding but perhaps we had more to thank Moiseyeva and Minenkov for—until the arrival of Chris and Jayne, that is. The Russian couple brought prestige to ice dance as part of the sport of figure skating. In his day, he confesses, it had been almost a joke, given little credence. Then Moiseyeva and Minenkov appeared with a completely different style and with an emphasis on choreography under the influence of the Bolshoi. Minenkov was underrated in the shadow of his beautiful and creative wife, but in Demmy's view he is the only skater who can be compared with Christopher Dean as an ice dance technician.

Although Pakhomova remains supreme among women ice dancers, Chris and Jayne are outstanding as a couple, brilliant individualists who achieve a blend and a feeling for each other's skating that is unequalled. 'People say they move as one, but it's almost got to a situation,' Demmy thinks, 'where if one of them

Diane Towler and Bernard Ford, predecessors to Chris and Jayne as holders of the world title (*All-Sport Photographic*)

makes a slight mistake the other one can almost match it at the same time so that it probably goes unnoticed. That's how they've perfected their unison. It's almost psychic, they can read each other's thoughts. I've never seen anything like it.'

Looking at our young champions individually, Demmy sees the improvement in Chris as 'phenomenal'. He has tremendous confidence now and has come to realise that he is a great ice dancer, both as a creator and as a performer. Jayne has made huge strides in all respects. Her appearance has improved, her personality has grown and from being a good technician she has emerged as a perfect partner for Chris. 'She always had a tremendous ability, but she didn't know what to do with it.' Chris had also been a little inhibited about doing some of the character movements needed to express different types of music, for example the samba. He would do a job, but it had been rather half-hearted.

Now 'he's got over that, with the help of several people connected with ballet and ballroom. He now knows there is nothing to be ashamed of in exaggerated body movements to sell a different type of dance. I could not live with the skaters of today because there is no way I could perform the body movements now needed to express the character of the music. In my day the compulsory dances represented 60% of the total marks; today it is only 30%. It is understandable therefore that the skaters concentrate their efforts on presentation and artistic impression which have become so important in the judging of OSP and free dance,' Demmy said.

Why, then, had he shrunk from giving Jayne and Chris 6.0 for *Mack and Mabel* at Nottingham in November 1981? 'I might have done it in the past where we were looking for a faultless performance according to the rules but now it has to be both faultless and perfect. I genuinely feel that, as beautiful as anything is, it could still perhaps be just that bit better.' Oddly enough, Chris and Jayne have made the point for him by their own brilliance. 'I have seen them go and skate in a way that I've thought was unbelievable, untouchable. Then they have gone out again and somehow been even better.' He was tempted to mark them with 6.0 at Lyons, when he was keeping a record as the referee, but he could not bring himself to do it. He was glad afterwards, believing he would see something even better at Copenhagen, but 'as it happens I was wrong. It may have been something to with the atmosphere at Copenhagen, since all artists respond to an audience.'

'Mack' and 'Mabel' bring their magic back from Copenhagen in March 1982 for a special performance as Astaire and Rogers 'Putting on the Ritz' at Richmond (*All-Sport Photographic*)

For that other judging Scrooge, Courtney Jones, there were two performances he could watch for ever (up to the autumn of 1982), John Curry's Olympic free at Innsbruck in 1976 and *Mack and Mabel*. Every time he watches *Mack and Mabel* on video he sees something he has previously missed. He recalls using the British couple's 1981 free dance for lecturing in Canada, yet the following year he came to regard it as 'old-fashioned, ridiculous as it may sound'. He thought at Hartford that they had reached the top too quickly. A year later he marvelled at the advance they had made 'with a totally new concept and the potential for progress that still seemed to be in them'.

Jones echoed Demmy's high regard for Pakhomova—'one of the best technicians of all time'—and Moiseyeva as an artist—'a creative skater, no great technician'. But Jayne, too, 'has become such a rounded, complete ice dancer. She is a marvellous anchor, always in the right place at the right time and that is an incredible ability. And she happens to have the right partner to complement her clever technical ability. She has developed a presence on the ice, learnt to show off, if you like. That's against her nature, but the moment it's over she reverts to her natural character, a sweet-natured girl who has remained exactly the same as when she first started. Chris, on the other hand, has become a much more confident young man, but he has always had a strong personality on the ice. He's now very capable of looking after himself, moving in high places with ease. You always know when he's in the room. I think he knows that it's part of his job to be seen and noticed.'

According to Bernard Ford, another former British world champion, 'watching them skate, the way they caress the ice, it's like watching God skate. They have been able to pull everything together and combine the strengths of so many people. Going back into the British heritage of skating, we have always been good skaters and always good dancers, but terribly upright in the body. There had not been a great deal of rhythm and musical motion. When the Russians came along their basic ingredient was the characterisation of the music. They may not have been so technically correct, lacking the ability to skate on edges and lobes [curves] and make patterns. Chris and Jayne have brought everything to it. They have shown that you can do the characterisation and the skating at an extreme of excellence at once go.'

They were, he thought, equally strong on either foot. If either had a weak foot he, or she, had worked on it so that there was no difference. 'You watch them attack the lobes. They turn left and right with equal facility, the lady sometimes on the right, sometimes on the left, which puts the pressure on the man on opposite feet, and the lady too. They do a lot of mirror steps, echo steps, switching of roles, or doing things on the opposite foot. They are, if I can coin a word, ambifootstrous! And there's such an affection there. You can't fake that sort of thing.'

One of the doubtful privileges of doing well in the world championships is to be drafted automatically into the ISU tour that follows for two to three weeks. There have been occasional defections for political reasons, but in the ordinary way a refusal would tend to damage one's reputation in the skating world. Chris and Jayne had already taken part in one such tour after their success at Hartford in 1981, but that rigorous experience was nothing to the trial that faced them in Europe after Copenhagen. In the United States and Canada much of the drudgery was spared them by a professional promotion team who provided outriders to smooth the way ahead, at airports and hotels particularly, and they were rarely required to carry their bags farther than across the threshold of their hotel rooms. In Europe they had to be their own porters and travelling dogsbodies, but Chris and Jayne, along with Scott Hamilton and Elaine Zayak, American winners of the individual titles, were the ones who suffered most.

The host of Russians and East Germans in the company would hardly have been disposed to complain about a venture that took them to so many western cities. Other westerners in the party were making their maiden voyages and would relish the novelty and the prestige. It was a glittering cast and a commercial impresario would have had to rob Fort Knox to drum up the cash needed to promote such a show. It is expensive to include one former world champion in a company, let alone four current world champions (six if you double the pairs and ice dancers), accompanied by their nearest challengers. They ought to have been treated with kid gloves; they ought not to have been herded around like unhappy tourists on a cheap tour. But they were.

For Chris and Jayne the depression started on the Monday after Copenhagen. By then most of the friendly faces of the skating fraternity had vanished—other skaters, coaches, judges, officials, press and groupies. Term was over and only a few people were still around to pick up the pieces. The competitions were behind them and the skaters, or at least those who had already been through the ISU mill, were anxious to go home to share their joy with family and friends, to bask in a glow of domestic and public adulation. Instead, they had to summon their determination to hit a high thirteen times in the span of a couple of weeks. The ISU are merely asking the skaters to put something back into a sport that has conferred such blessings on them. That may not be unreasonable, but both the

The prototype, the pose and the performance: Chris and Jayne, who enjoy Astaire–Rogers films, were encouraged by the *Daily Mail* to dress for the part and from that project they developed an Astaire–Rogers exhibition that forms part of their present extensive repertoire (*Chris Barham/ Daily Mail; All-Sport Photographic*)

programme and promotion of the 1982 tour made unfair demands.

The tour began in Moscow, scarcely the most warm and hospitable starting point. There were the usual frustrations suffered by all visitors to the Soviet Union—a long queue here for a bus, there for a document, somewhere else for a key. When, eventually, Chris walked into his room he was pursued by a lad anxious to buy jeans, training shoes and other items of supposed luxury in the west. They were in Moscow for three days and were then rushed off by night train to Leningrad straight from the show. 'That was ridiculous,' Jayne complains. 'We didn't need an extra day in Moscow. All told, we had only four free days. The others were in Prague, in Dortmund when the tour was over and we all wanted to get home, and in Bordeaux, which at least was a nice break.'

Moscow was not unmitigated torment. The skating conditions were superb, the crowd large and responsive, the rink facilities excellent. A projected tour of Red Square and Lenin's tomb had to be abandoned because it was a day of some trade union celebration or other, but for the privileged few there was a trip to the Bolshoi. Here something extraordinary happened, which would have a special significance the following season. Chris, one of the five who were offered a ticket for the Bolshoi, exchanged his with Brian Pockar, of Canada, for a ticket to the state circus. What could be in his mind, Jayne wondered to herself at the time?

All skaters appreciate the movement and music of the ballet, from John Curry downwards, yet here was a leading exponent passing up the chance for a view of clowns, trapeze artists, jugglers, tightrope walkers, etc. Bolshoi tickets are like gold dust. During the Olympic Games in 1980 I had somehow acquired two tickets surplus to my requirements and disposed of them at the door of the theatre in circumstances that recalled the distribution of Red Cross parcels in another kind of theatre—to two German nurses at that. There would be a touch of irony the following summer when Chris proposed to go to Verona, with Jayne, in order to catch the Bolshoi and was prevented at the last minute by a foot injury.

The big top

Bit by bit the secret of Chris's rejection of the Bolshoi leaked out among a circle of friends, though never to the press or general public. Casting around for something to measure up to *Mack and Mabel*, he had hit upon a circus theme. He and Jayne had at one time considered an Astaire-Rogers programme, partly inspired by a photographic session arranged by the *Daily Mail* where they were dressed to represent two of their cinema favourites, but the idea was scotched by Judy Blumberg and Michael Seibert. The Americans used Astaire–Rogers for their free dance at Copenhagen, having been forced to abandon their original programme as inadequate in the light of reports from Europe of the wholesale surrender of judges to *Mack and Mabel*. An exhibition that Chris and Jayne evolved to 'Putting on the Ritz', first seen during the ISU tour, was taking shape before they had seen Blumberg and Seibert, so the suspicion held in some quarters that they had drawn their idea from the Americans was completely false.

During the ISU tour they had acquired a French tape of *Barnum*, a hit show both in New York and London. The fact that they hardly understood a word was irrelevant. It was the music that mattered— vocals are not allowed in skating competitions, as distinct from exhibitions—and that appealed to them strongly. Back in England they consulted Courtney Jones because Betty Callaway was away on holiday and received a positive response. Through the manager of the Theatre Royal, Nottingham, they procured four tickets for *Barnum* at the Palladium for themselves, Jones and Thompson.

The public recognition they now enjoyed was clear from the press of autograph hunters, but they had also been surreptitiously recognised by the star, indeed the life and soul, of *Barnum*. He was Michael Crawford, who peeped behind the curtain at the interval and spotted the two young people whose work he had so much admired on the television screen. The theatre manager then brought them a message asking if they would like to go backstage when the show finished. So an hour or so later 'these two huge grins came through the door' in the words of Michael Crawford himself. 'With me as well,' he said later, 'we must have looked like the Channel tunnel.'

They took to each other straight away. Chris and Jayne found that Michael Crawford was a fan of theirs and of *Mack and Mabel* in particular; and they, for their part, were in the palm of his hand from the moment he bounded on to the stage. From the start they were on first-name terms, and when they expressed an interest in using the music from *Barnum* for their next programme Michael felt 'thrilled and flattered. Chris asked me if there was a record without me singing. "Nothing personal", he added, "but we're not allowed to use voices". I didn't know that. I just thought my voice offended him. Unfortunately there is no overture to *Barnum*. They endeared themselves to me so much that I was determined to see if something could be done.' By the time the evening was finished Jones and Thompson had virtually designed the costumes.

A few weeks later Chris was exercising on a rowing machine—'an instrument of torture' in Jayne's view that he and she had installed in the Torvill garden—when a call came from Michael Crawford. Chris had almost given up hope of anything developing from the Palladium meeting. His brain was slow to pick up the name but when the penny dropped he rushed into the house breathless with excitement. Michael wanted to reassure them that he had not forgotten them, that he had himself been unwell and that the man he had to contact had been away. He expected to let them know something more positive soon, but if they wanted to visit the Palladium again in the meantime he would be delighted to renew their acquaintance. Nothing could have been nearer to their thoughts than another view of *Barnum* and this time they were accompanied by Betty Callaway.

The missions to the Palladium provide an interesting footnote to history, for it had once been an ice stadium. In 1896 Hengler's Circus, an elaborate theatre in Argyll Street near London's Oxford Circus, was converted into the National Skating Palace and became the headquarters of the NSA. The third world championships, a modest affair in those days accommodating only four men solo skaters, were held there in 1898. The theatre was re-established in 1910 as the London Palladium.

Chris's first idea was that the original tapes used for the show, without the vocal accompaniment, might still be available, but this proved not to be the case. However, Michael Crawford came up with a mind-blowing suggestion: why not have the music specially written and recorded for them? It was an ambitious project, quite beyond their imagination, but Michael knew that the musical director of the show, Michael Reed, would be willing to cooperate.

Reed joined the three of them and Betty Callaway in the dressing-room after the show this time and was quick to offer his services free in scoring four minutes from the show. He would be able to arrange a studio for the recording, but most of the musicians would have to be paid. They all left the Palladium that night with their minds in a

The London Palladium during its period as an ice rink at the turn the century (*J. R. C. Yglesias*)

whirl. They were now moving into a new league, where they could command precisely what music they wanted and how they wanted it performed. They were, however, facing a bill of £1,000 or so.

There was one particular drawback about *Barnum*. Chris and Jayne had already thought of a device for simulating the trapeze on ice and needed a waltz for that purpose, something that the show lacked. They were contemplating filling the gap with music from elsewhere, but Michael Reed convinced them that he could adapt a piece from the show to waltz time. Both Michaels were concerned about the copyright because Sir Harry Fielding owned the rights in the United Kingdom and kept jealous guard of his possession. He had refused permission for Cy Coleman's music to be used on a variety of occasions, once even after a film had been made for showing on television. This hurdle was safely crossed, with Sir Harry's blessing—even his good wishes—and it was now all systems go.

Michael Crawford later confessed that his mind was also in a whirl. The whole project had caught his imagination so much that he was keen to become totally involved, yet he was aware of Betty Callaway's position as the skaters' trainer. 'I didn't know how people functioned in the skating world,' he said, 'and I didn't want to tread on "Henry's" toes.' It has to be explained that his use of her own first name tended to cause some embarrassment, since the use of 'Betty' induced him automatically to lapse into the chaotic character of Frank Spencer in the British television comedy series *Some mothers do 'ave 'em*, whose long-suffering wife was also called Betty.

'Henry' does not suit Betty Callaway's personality at all, but it was the imaginative touch you might expect from such a gifted performer. 'Henry', unselfish person that she is, did not mind in the least and they were to form a formidable team of four in their search for something worthy to follow *Mack and Mabel*. Chris and Jayne were in Oberstdorf at the time of the studio recording, but they had taken with them a tape of the music they wanted performed on piano by Michael Reed. They were able to begin to put their programme together when the time came for one of them to fly home for the recording. The choice fell upon Jayne, as Chris explains:

❛I can be too easily pleased with music. Jayne's more critical about what she wants and if I'd come back with a piece of music which she didn't like I'd have to put up with her for the rest of the time. She wants the music exact, whereas I tend to think too quickly 'oh, that'll do'. I had to press her into going, because she had never before travelled alone on a journey like that and didn't fancy the idea. ❜

After a night with Betty Callaway at Beaconsfield, conveniently near London airport, Jayne and Betty went to the studio the next morning. They were surprised and delighted to discover that the enthusiastic Michael Crawford was there, too. For Jayne, it was a memorable occasion:

❛I was amazed. There must have been twelve musicians there tuning up, all at my command! I just felt like nobody walking in there but I was made to seem like somebody very special, whose every wish had to be met. They were all there just because we wanted them to play our music. But really Mike Reed was the man in charge. He got everything moving and we just stood back. They did the tracks separately, one for the strings, one for piano, one for percussion etc. As I listened I couldn't possibly tell what the whole picture would be like until the end and it was embarrassing when Mike kept asking if this or that sounded OK. Some pieces were easy, like the slow section when there were only two instruments, but others made little sense to me at that fragmented stage. Mike would keep asking 'how does that sound?' and sometimes it was difficult for me to reply without showing my ignorance in a field which he, of course, took for granted.

It took longer than expected and we had to return the next day for the balancing of the various tapes, which added to the £1,000 estimate of the cost. We met at a different studio the next day, the other one having already been booked, and there was this technician, a real expert, pushing these slides on a console up and down in order to get the exact effect he, and we, wanted. When it was finished it sounded fabulous. I was thrilled. We can never thank Mike Reed enough for all he did for us. He must have spent eight hours in the studio on the first day and four or five on the second, quite apart from all the trouble he had taken at other times. He was a perfectionist, too, often going after another improvement even when I'd said I was satisfied. The score was apparently difficult and one or two session musicians had declined the engagement, specially trumpet players. The extra day, plus air fares, pushed the cost near to £1,500.

Jayne came away from the recording studio walking on air, with two cassettes for herself and another for Michael Crawford, which she delivered that same afternoon to the Palladium. Even on a battered old cassette player that Michael kept in his dressing-room 'Barnum on ice', as it was officially called, sounded 'marvellous', according to Jayne. Why had Michael Crawford, with so much already on his plate, become so engrossed in what Jayne and Chris were trying to do? He said later:

6 I loved their dedication apart from admiring them as performers. They're a very charming couple and we got on well from the moment we met, every one of us. It wasn't simply because we were in my dressing-room, on a high after the show. We were the same later when we went up to Peterborough for a try-out. We were sitting at the bar upstairs, going crazy.

I'm not sure about my use of the word dedication. It's like saying they're workaholics, and that's an insult to someone who enjoys his work. They're perfectionists, trying to achieve the best to be the best. Otherwise they'd be wasting one enormous talent. Jayne glows, she glows. She's got a smile that can charm the birds from the trees. Beautiful personality on the ice. Chris is a brilliant young man for his years. He has all the determination and eagerness that it takes to be the best. We had great fun and I wanted to be one of the team, if Betty Callaway would let me. 9

Chris was at Munich airport to meet Jayne, Betty and their treasured cargo, when they arrived back from London and could hardly wait to pack the bags into the car and slot the cassette into place. They played it over and over again on the two-hour journey to Oberstdorf, discussing the characteristics of each section. It 'sounded great', Chris says, but:

6 The way I'd originally cut it, there were differences between the makeshift piano recording and the new music. We'd already got the whole programme practically finished after a month and a half with piano. When this version came back and I went through the steps in my mind while it was playing, I realised that some changes had been

made. Jayne knew, of course, and was watching my face to see how I reacted, so I discovered afterwards. It was no big worry. More serious was the fact that the music had been expanded from four minutes on the nose, the ISU requirement, to four minutes ten seconds, which was right on the borderline of what they would allow. When we got to the rink we speeded it up to about four minutes eight or nine, which may sound nothing but it made a big difference. We wanted it under four minutes ten for safety, because that's the absolute limit. If we went beyond that we would be penalised.

An unexpec'ed new problem arose when they played the tape in the Oberstdoii rink, because certain sections sounded flat on the public address system. Jayne had not been able to detect the flaw in the studio nor was it apparent in the car, but now the sound level in the vast area of rink seemed to waver, taking them to a big build-up and falling away. Jayne was growing more despondent with every passing minute, having spent so much time and trouble in London putting the tape together. She had returned to Oberstdorf convinced that a prayer had been answered and now suffered this crushing disappointment. It was short-lived, because a telephone call to Michael Reed put their minds at rest. The tape could easily be rebalanced when they returned home, though it was to take another four hours before they got it right. They had now moved into a new field of sophisticated ice dance, with music recorded according to their own specification. It was yet another example of their not being satisfied with conventional methods. If there was a way forward, they would want to find it.

The new tape was prepared on a quick trip home for shows at Bournemouth. This was an interesting new commercial venture, which was not entirely successful, although there were full houses when Chris and Jayne were appearing. But they could meet only four of their six engagements, because of a bizarre accident suffered by Chris on the way to the rink on the last day. He tripped over an uneven paving stone and cracked the fifth metatarsal of his right foot, the long bone running down to the little toe. Jayne showed little sympathy (they do not have too much tolerance of the other's various ailments) and was more amused than anything else as Chris hopped about the pavement.

'I thought I'd frighten him,' she said later. 'I said let's ring the hospital and arrange an x-ray, and expected him to pooh-pooh the idea, but he agreed immediately. I realised then that he'd done himself a mischief.' The injury proved to be more serious than the sprain they had first diagnosed and the local hospital provided not only a strapping but also a pair of crutches. He would not be able to skate for a month and certainly would not be fit for a projected visit to the Bolshoi in Italy *en route* for more exhibitions and training at Morzine. Chris discarded the crutches after a week and gingerly put blade to ice after twelve days at Morzine. It was the longest period they had been off the ice since they had been skating together. Betty Callaway was quite undisturbed by the injury. She was aware how hard they had worked on *Barnum* and regarded the enforced rest as beneficial, given the trivial nature of the injury.

The break enabled them to bend their minds to the rock 'n' roll OSP, which the ISU had sprung on the ice dance world that year as a test of their ingenuity. There was so little precise recognition of rock 'n' roll that the ISU were forced to issue an explanatory note that did little to clear away the fog. It said that the tempo had been deliberately left unrestricted as most rock 'n' roll music had been produced as vocal music and therefore it would not be easy to find good music. They hoped they would not have to suffer twenty-five renditions of 'Rock around the clock'. Rock 'n' roll could also include skating movements and music that embraced the jive and swing. It was not up to the ice dance committee to tell skaters what to do. They would have to use their own imagination.

Chris and Jayne had included jive numbers in their previous free dances and had thought that rock 'n' roll would be something of a pushover, but it did not come at all easily. They had some ideas— they are never without them—but they just could not make them work with the pattern that was in their mind. As usual, they ignored the easy options, perhaps the only source of encouragement was the thought that the harder they worked in the creation the more effective would be the end product. They hammered out the OSP in the month they were at Morzine where there was a small rink, and returned to Oberstdorf for two weeks.

They needed to keep the OSP and free on a tight rein because the Nottingham rink, where they would first perform them in the British championship in November, was twelve feet smaller both in length and width. The rink at Morzine, approximately the same size as Nottingham, had been perfect for laying down the pattern and was chosen for that purpose. It would be easy to expand it later on the bigger rinks in Dortmund and Helsinki for the European and world championships respectively. At Oberstdorf they marked the ice to bring the area they used down to that of the Nottingham rink. Chris believes that training on a small rink is an advantage, partly because it makes for stronger edges. Moving to a smaller rink calls for an adjustment that can affect harmony. It might be too small for detection by outside eyes, but they are aware of the tiniest deviation. Chris:

❛It takes us about four or five days to feel comfortable on a small rink after training on a larger one. After the first week to week and a half we are pushing out as much as we would normally on a big rink, but still staying within the bounds. It's a funny thing, hard to explain. You would naturally think that if you're pushing as hard as before you would be overdoing it, but you learn to sense where the barriers are. ❜

They had hit upon the music for the rock 'n' roll, partly by luck and partly by refusing to consider the Bill Haley cliché. Their search had seemed to lead them nowhere, when they happened to be sitting together in the audience of *Song and Dance*, a London show of Andrew Lloyd Webber's music featuring the singer Marti Webb in the first half and the dancer Wayne Sleep in the second. The show was almost over when Sleep and his company went into a rock 'n' roll sequence to the music of Paganini, adapted by Lloyd Webber, the man who has brought new life to the British musical scene with such shows as *Jesus Christ Superstar*, *Evita* and *Cats*. Within a few seconds Chris and Jayne turned to each other with raised eyebrows and meaningful looks. Here was exactly what they had been looking for—a fresh piece of music, with no lyrics, that was almost tailored to their needs. Subsequent events tended to strengthen its appeal. The record of the show was not then available and by the time it was—in August—there was no likelihood of another couple having chosen it.

The St Ivel competition at Richmond loomed, but it had already been decided by Betty Callaway and the two skaters that *Barnum* would not follow *Mack and Mabel* on to that particular stage. There would be world-wide curiosity about what they would be doing to surpass *Mack and Mabel* and they did not feel like unveiling it five or six months before the world championships. Three peaks in one season would be enough. In any case, both the free and the rock 'n' roll were demanding technically as well as physically and they would not feel ready for the St Ivel. Those spectators would have to make do with *Mack and Mabel*, Astaire–Rogers, *Kiss me Kate* and their sublime rumba. That was a feast enough there for any couple, but they were not just any couple. They had made themselves unique.

The NSA and St Ivel, the sponsoring company, accepted with good grace that they might be asking too much and readily agreed to settle for exhibitions from the world champions. With Blumberg and Seibert, Barber and Slater and a strong supporting cast in their competition, there would be no lack of quality in the ice dance. Chris and Jayne were conscious of the comparisons that would be made between their marks and performances in 1981–2 and 1982–3. Chris:

❝Striving to top what we've done before is a good aim for us on one hand, a frightening one on the other. Anybody who is competing is not going to say deliberately that he doesn't have to do better than the year before. Every time Daley Thompson competes he is trying to beat his own decathlon record if the conditions are right. He doesn't say to himself 'it's going to be a walkover this year. I don't have to bust a gut'. It's a personal thing.

But with us it's so different, with no stopwatch or tape measure to provide a test. It's like judging an actor. We don't worry about the pressure in the light of the marks the previous year. We want to do it for ourselves. We don't want to feel 'that's it, that's as far as we can go'. We feel we can go a bit further if we work at it. People have said of some skaters that they introduced a certain thing to the sport, people like John Curry, Moiseyeva and Minenkov, Pakhomova, Rodnina and Zaitsev. It must be nice if, when you finish, you can say to yourself that at least you left a mark. That's our ultimate aim. ❞

Judy Blumberg and Michael Seibert, the American champions, skating their rock 'n' roll OSP at Richmond, September 1982 (*All-Sport Photographic*)

The distinctions came thick and fast in the winter of 1982. They were again chosen as Team of the Year by the Sports Writers' Association, a remarkable achievement since many members of that body do not even acknowledge skating, particularly ice dance, as sport at all. They believe that no activity that depends on human evaluation can be so regarded; at best it is one man's view against another, rather like choosing a champion dog or cat, at worst prone to prejudice, domestic and international. For them, a tape measure or stopwatch has to be brought to bear, or a record of how many goals or points are scored.

Yet figure skating has an honourable place in the history of sport. It was represented at that historic meeting called by Baron de Coubertin in Paris in 1894 to revive the Olympic Games and was originally included in the programme for the first Games in 1900. In fact, it had to wait eight more years until the old Prince's Club at Knightsbridge, London, offered a suitable setting. Ice dancing, however, came later to the scene and was included in the Olympic Games for the first time in 1976. Since then it has tended to overshadow pair skating, both as a competitive discipline and public spectacle. On this occasion Jayne was not dismayed to be superseded as Sportswoman of the Year. She had not felt she had won it on her own in 1981, anyway. 'We won it together,' she declares.

This was a happy introduction to the British championship of 1982, an event that was to leave Chris and Jayne a little bewildered and disappointed. The secrecy over *Barnum* seemed to develop a momentum of its own. There was no serious intention from the first of hiding away from prying eyes, but at no time did it seem the right moment to talk about it openly. They were subjected to the greatest curiosity about their intentions almost from the time they came back from the ISU tour the previous March. The whole skating world wondered how they could possibly find a successor to *Mack and Mabel* that would not seem an anti-climax.

From quietly resisting inquiries in the formative period they became convinced that they would hold their peace until the last minute. They are not given to talking much about themselves and their activities; they tend to go their own way, keeping themselves to themselves. Training at Oberstdorf and Morzine contributed to the process of isolation and when the season reopened, they had become conditioned to fending off inquiries about their new programme. From there it was a small step to deciding to break the news only on the eve of the championship at Nottingham.

Although they still did not show their hand on the ice, they held a press conference on the day before the championship, a meeting that grew from a small intimate gathering of two or three regular

Along with their stunning advances in other areas of ice dance, Torvill and Dean have brought a new intensity of emotion to their characterisation of different forms of music; here, with jealous rage in her eyes, Jayne frustrates Chris's attempt to escape from her clutches (*Eileen Langsley/Supersport Photographs*)

reporters of ice skating to almost a score of journalists crushed into a room kindly put at their disposal by the manager of the Old Cricket Players public house opposite the rink. Their number included the London correspondent of the Moscow newspaper, *Trud*, Mr Alexei Burmistenko, a charming man who provided a wholly acceptable alternative to the video camera that had so angered Betty Callaway at Richmond the previous year on the début of *Mack and Mabel* on ice. The intention of the press conference was to explain exactly what they were doing for their free dance and OSP and to acknowledge publicly the help they had received from the two Michaels, Crawford and Reed. With photographs arranged by Crawford's press agent, the British ice dance championship of 1982 was launched with unparalleled publicity.

The photographs revealed how Michael Crawford had gone to Peterborough to cooperate in the preparation of the free dance. His presence at the rink was a daunting experience. It was the first time they formally offered *Barnum* for inspection to anybody outside their coterie of confidants. It had something of the flavour of a first night in the theatre, although there was an audience of scarcely a dozen people, mostly skaters now turned fascinated spectators. It was much more nerve-racking than their first showing of *Mack and Mabel* to Mary Parry and Roy Mason, because of Michael Crawford's reputation and because they were under such pressure this time to improve on a performance that had drawn eight 6.0s out of nine in the European championship for artistic impression.

By now they had lived with *Barnum* for so long that they were unable to see the wood for the trees. Their critical faculties had been dulled by constant repetition and they needed an outside opinion, the view of somebody seeing it for the first time. They were mightily pleased with the response, since Crawford's delight was patently sincere. There was a last chance of declaring their hand publicly at the official practice on the morning of the championship, but they still held back. Having come so far, they might as well go the whole hog and aim for greater impact in the evening. They later doubted the wisdom of that decision.

The championship opened with fresh departures from tradition, new evidence of original thinking. Chris, Jayne and Betty Callaway had now formed the view that the compulsory dances need not be totally devoid of individual character. For all the rigidity of the ISU rules there was some leeway for personal expression. They not only introduced subtle variations of the Ravensburger waltz and the Argentine tango but even made changes from one sequence to the next in each dance. They hoped thereby to make the dances more interesting for ordinary spectators. Their marks touched 5.9 at one

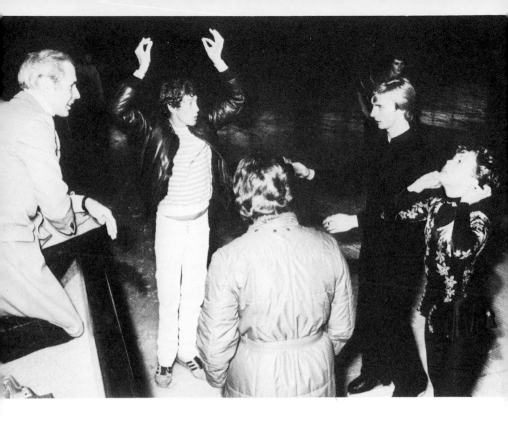

Courtney Jones (left) and Betty Callaway are interested spectators as Michael Crawford introduces Chris and Jayne to circus techniques at Peterborough (*Doug McKenzie/Professional Photographic Services*)

point and fell to 5.5 at another, as in 1981, but whereas on that occasion there were eight 5.5s, now there was only one, from Joan Noble. There was a solitary 5.9 in both events. A 6.0 is almost without precedent in the compulsories. Their average mark was nearly 5.7, compared with 5.65 a year earlier and the graph of improvement was still rising.

The evening carried the same heady atmosphere as the year before, though for a different reason. In 1981, for all *Mack and Mabel*'s winning way in the St Ivel, the excitement had been generated more by their return home as world champions for the first time. That was an unrepeatable experience, but in its place was the stimulus of emulating their previous year's blockbuster. A minor demonstration was held outside the rink to protest against the fur trade, since the event was sponsored by Sovereign Furs, but fears that there would be disruption within—with live television and Chris and Jayne the chief magnets for protesters seeking publicity—proved to be unfounded. To a large extent expectations of the rock 'n' roll OSP had been overshadowed by those of the free but Chris and Jayne immediately brought it to the centre of the stage with a virtuoso performance. It was, for them, the highlight of the evening, as Jayne explains:

❛We were more apprehensive about the OSP than the free dance, because it was harder to do, both physically and technically. Nowhere was there a rest in it, and nobody does three and a half minutes' fast skating in a free dance. Three minutes is as much as you want for an OSP, especially one as demanding as that, but we could find no suitable places to cut the music, so we could not really shorten it. We got no rest. It was steps, steps, steps all the way. It was the best OSP we had ever done. We were thrilled with the way it went and the reception it got. ❜

They had sweated blood to get that OSP into shape, with two barriers to surmount, first the intricacy of the test they had set themselves on the ice and then the demands on their bodies and lungs. The progression was first to get the individual pieces to work, then to link them together. They put the first half of the sequence together, they polished off the second half and then they had, in Chris's words, to 'crack the whole sequence'. Eventually, they got beyond the first sequence and went straight from there to the whole performance. They found that when they had completed two sequences their collective wills flowed automatically into the third.

When they had shown it at Peterborough there had been flattering comments about its brilliant construction but criticism of the timing. That had not worried them because they find at championships that they are so excited at the start of the week in training sessions that they are usually ahead of themselves, creating an illusion that the recording is too slow. It takes a day or two to adapt. The dance was notable for the twists imposed on Jayne's arms and shoulders. The highlight, placed strategically in the centre of the rink, requires Chris to 'unwrap' Jayne in a lateral twist lying just above the ice, a masterpiece of invention, of adaptability to the character of rock 'n' roll and of timing as Jayne surfaces with left foot on the beat. Were they satisfied with the final product? Chris:

❛We certainly were. Most people won't remember it as, if you want to use the word, a classic, like the blues of the previous season. It was completely the opposite and confirmed, we like to think, our versatility. With a fast OSP it always is going to live or die by its technical excellence, by how difficult and exciting you can make it. I don't think anybody could possibly have said that we'd gone off. ❜

Devoted Torvill-Dean supporters declare their faith at all their competition performances (*All-Sport Photographic*)

In designing outfits for the OSP Courtney Jones had had to take notice of an ISU document which points out: 'Naturally the skaters feel the need to wear costumes which help to create the right mood. That's understandable and acceptable, but we are staging a sport and not exhibitions or ice revues. The rule says dress must be modest and dignified.' Jones put them both in simple tee-shirts bearing the initials 'CJ', not as a form of self-advertisement for the designer but to identify the wearers, as was common practice when rock 'n' roll held sway in the dance halls. They both wore a red scarf, Chris a pair of black trousers and Jayne a pretty black billowing skirt with a full white underskirt. They looked and played the part to perfection. There was almost complete uniformity among the judges—apart from some reservations about the music—with only three departures from 5.9: the 5.8 of Courtney Jones for presentation and the 6.0 from Brenda Long and Roy Mason for the same element. It is an interesting commentary on human evaluation that whereas all three judges held the same view as to technical merit (or composition, as it is termed in the OSP), one judge felt that they fell away in the presentation whereas two others felt they were 'faultless and perfect'. The champions had achieved no 6.0s for 'Summertime' at Nottingham and Lawrence Demmy's two 5.9s were an encouraging advance on his 5.6 and 5.7 in 1981.

If only the evening had ended there. The free was no great disaster, merely a lapse from the absolute perfection they demanded of themselves and it gnawed at their self-esteem. They could not have foreseen the discomfort that would assail them all too soon as they took their opening pose for *Barnum*—left arms bowed on hips, right arms extended. They were clad in white: Chris with a sparkling blue cravat front, Jayne with a matching waistband and black choker; a handsome blend of chic and show-biz.

By any normal standards what followed was another splendid performance running through the gamut of a circus: the juggling was transparently clear, providing you happened to have an effective vantage point, behind the judges for instance; so were the hazardous tightrope walk and the making up of the clowns, followed by the donning of the huge trousers so beloved of that fraternity; the trapeze was a charming interlude and there was an invitation to follow the band, evoked by a cute impression of trombone-playing.

Then to a rousing finish. Interspersed with these and other routine circus highlights were a number of trick movements, simulating those performed by clowns to divert attention from the centre of the action where mundane transformations were being wrought by men in blue overalls. These gave Chris and Jayne the opportunity to display their inventiveness, notably when Jayne sweeps a circle of ice

Chris and Jayne performing their stylish Argentine tango in the British championship at Nottingham 1982 (*Colorsport*)

Barnum unveiled at last at Nottingham 1982 (*Colorsport*)

with one foot apparently in defiance of the other three. That became something of a trade-mark like the side-steps on points by Jayne draped over her partner's back first introduced in *Mack and Mabel*.

Apart from one stumble by Jayne, her concentration perhaps impaired by personal unease, the performance went down well and there was another storming ovation. Not one of the eighteen marks fell below 5.9, and there was even a 6.0. All this was accomplished only because of the thorough preparation that had gone into their training. Jayne's dress, which had looked a picture in her sitting-room mirror, could not stand up to the strain of four acrobatic minutes—for which neither the designer nor the dress-maker was to blame—and she was disturbed by the possibility of it slipping from one shoulder or the other. Even so, they do not advance that as an excuse for a performance which left them downcast, however much it may have satisfied judges and public.

They were under an unprecedented spotlight of publicity and would be bound to proceed with some caution, to start with at least. They would have a chance to let themselves go later if they felt everything was clicking into place. 'But it wasn't there that night,' Chris explains. 'Whereas normally we can walk confidently along a thin edge, this time we were staggering along, hoping to stay upright.' They must have felt that their simulation of a perilous wire-walk in *Barnum*, culminating in a quick clutch by Chris to prevent Jayne from apparently falling, held an unintentional hint of self-parody.

In the circumstances, the champions found it hard to raise a smile at a reception later in the evening. To make matters worse, they had been unable to contact Michael Crawford and the two sides had to wait until the morning to compare notes. Michael had hurried through *his* performance of *Barnum* in order to be back in the dressing-room to watch the ice dancing live on BBC television. He did not share their despondency, indeed was still bubbling with enthusiasm the next morning. He was anxious to get to work on improvements immediately, unable perhaps to grasp the fact that they now needed to stand off a little, to come down from the 'high' they had built up for the British. That, coupled with a new honour bestowed on them by way of the BBC, meant they did not resume contact with Michael Crawford for a month. His support continued on the same high plane.

The judges, as their marks showed, were delighted with the dish that had been put before them. That one stumble was enough to deter them from hoisting a 6.0, except in one isolated instance, but they would have welcomed an opportunity to see the programme in practice during the morning. They would have been better able then to appreciate the various constituent parts in the evening and clear their minds of possible transgressions of the rules, in the matter of lifts for instance. The following morning, however, they gave the programme the green light.

More material expressions of approval came from members of the public. Their swelling postbag after Nottingham included a number of touching gifts, none more so than a gold sovereign from a lady in her eightieth year. She doubted, she said, if she would need it much longer. Another lady sent a pair of doves, having been left with an image of birds in flight by their white-suited movements on the ice. Other gifts included a clown in a white costume with a blue frill to match Jayne's dress and a little perfumed harlequin doll for hanging in her wardrobe. They were happy to send back letters of thanks, though their fan mail was reaching embarrassing proportions. Letters asking for a photograph could be readily dealt with, but those seeking to discuss technique, music, etc imposed a strain on their time and on Jayne's secretarial resources.

A new distinction in November 1982 was the issue of the overture

Winners of the BBC Sports Review of 1982 awards, (from left) Chris and Jayne (team), Daley Thompson (individual), Sir Garfield Sobers who presented the awards, Alex Higgins (second) and Steve Cram (third) (*BBC*)

The BBC converted an adjoining studio into an ice rink to enable Chris and Jayne to perform live during their Sports Review of 1982 programme (*BBC*)

to *Mack and Mabel* as a single record, in a sleeve bearing a photograph of Chris and Jayne. At the same time a reissue of the album of the show was achieving a success in the 'nostalgia' releases that must be seen as a tribute to their free dance, even when allowance is made for regular plugs on the BBC. The following month they were chosen the Team of the Year by BBC viewers and thus became the housewives' choice as well as the hard-bitten critics' choice. The BBC went further by setting up a small rink in the studio next to the one used for their 'Sports Review of 1982' programme. It covered an area of only 60 feet by 40 feet, hardly sufficient to see them at anything like their best, but enough for them to display several sleights of foot lifted mostly from the rock 'n' roll OSP. The year ended on a high note. Ahead lay a month or more of serious work before the first challenge to their superiority, the European championships at Dortmund in the first week of February 1983—as they then thought.

The greatest show on ice

There seemed to be some kind of jinx over the European championships at Dortmund. There was a drama about Chris's suit for *Barnum*, which needed some adjustments and was lost in the post between two London suburbs—Walthamstow where it had been made by Chris's tailor and Twickenham where Jayne's dressmaker, Sylvia Parish, lives. Chris was about to get into his car to leave for Heathrow and Oberstdorf at eight o'clock one morning in January when the telephone rang and he learnt that the suit had been found. A friend at Heathrow (they seem to have friends everywhere) provided a room where Chris could have a new fitting.

This little episode had loomed large over the normal tribulations of preparing for a month or so away from home, first at Oberstdorf and then Dortmund, with all the equipment they have to take with them. It was made to seem like a pinprick compared with the greater disaster that was to overtake them almost as soon as they got to Oberstdorf. They spent a day settling in and had star-billing on television as spectators of the German championships which were held that week at Oberstdorf. Then they took a day getting used to the ice, before they went into full training. Two days later their hopes were shattered by a fall which left Jayne a crumpled heap on the ice.

They were running through their revised free programme for the first time when they were poleaxed on the first lift after approximately ten seconds. They had devised a daring new lift to replace the cartwheel which had opened the British championship. Jayne had to throw herself backwards in a horizontal plane at shoulder height with a half-twist that brought her round to face the ceiling. At the same time Chris was travelling backwards and had to perform a complementary half-twist to face the front. They had done it well enough in practice but this time Chris was hauled forward off balance and there was no support for Jayne as she plunged to the ice. A friend who was watching said she was 'horrified' and feared a serious injury. Let Chris tell the story:

❝Everything looked dandy that Wednesday. We did our normal compulsory practice in the morning and at lunchtime the OSP rock 'n' roll. In the afternoon it was the free in the third hall, that is the second full-size rink in the Oberstorf complex. We were doing the new lift for the first time in a full run-through. We had developed it without music, of course, and then had done that section with music to get the timing right, but this was the first time that we set out with it as part of the full programme. It was a good lift, new and unusual, but this time we just wiped out. Jayne came down from five feet to zero on her back.

I had not regarded it as a dangerous lift from the point of view of possibly falling over, only that it was hard for Jayne because she landed on a running edge of her right foot in a sit position, with the left leg thrown forward behind the right. This time she went up, I turned and I could not stand up as her momentum pulled me forward. As I stumbled on to my stomach I tried to keep her head off the ice by pulling her hands up as far as I could and I may have twisted her right arm. I did not take too serious a view of it at the time. I thought it was only a tumble—a hard tumble because she did go down with quite a force. I quite expected we would be able to carry on, but when I helped her up and took her to the barrier she complained that her right leg was numb and she felt sick, ready to throw up.

I knew then she must have been severely shaken because she's a brave girl who does not make a fuss over nothing. Whenever a new move is suggested, either by me or someone else, she never ducks it on grounds of safety. Unless she thinks it impracticable she does it without a second thought. Even in this case, as soon as she was better some days later we went out and did it straight away, like a diver who's belly-flopped from the highboard or a showjumper who's messed up a big spread. On that afternoon she said she could not carry on and I took her back through the complex to her room, which fortunately is under the same roof. Halfway round she began to cry and I knew the pain had got to her.   ,

By the time a car had been summoned to take Jayne to the hospital she realised that the injury was more extensive than she had at first thought:

❛As I got into the car I felt my shoulder aching and by the time they started taking the x-rays my arm was killing me. The x-rays showed no broken bones, thank heavens, but it was some time before they were convinced about the shoulder, because of a line on the plate. I insisted that I had fallen on my side rather than the shoulder, which had been supported by Chris as he fell forward. The doctor, Hans Rohde, was wonderfully attentive and it was thanks to him and his staff, who opened the hospital specially for my benefit on Sunday, that I was able to make the recovery as quickly as I did. Dr Rohde came to visit me that evening and applied some cream to the tender parts. He gave me tablets for the inflammation and a sleeping pill, but I got no sleep that night. I could not find a position that did not cause some pain somewhere.

Chris brought me my tea, breakfast and whatever else I wanted. He even helped me to undress. I could not lift my arm up and he had to be a sort of general nursemaid. As well as the arm, I could not bend down to take my trousers off, nor could I bend my leg up. I felt so helpless. Getting out of bed and going to the loo was a major exercise taking half an hour. I could only limp, or kind of shuffle. I was really stiff for about three days before the pain began to die down. **9**

After three days Jayne was able to get on the ice, with Dr Rohde's approval, but it was little more than a token effort, because her right leg still protested at any extra effort. After five days she was able to move to a little better purpose, with Chris still fretting at the delay like a racehorse waiting for the off. A week after the fall (a Wednesday) they were able to get more or less into full swing, with four hours on the ice, avoiding the most energetic movements that might set back Jayne's recovery. The one movement they could not consider attempting was the horizontal twist in the rock 'n' roll, which placed great strain on Jayne's shoulders in pulling her back to the vertical. Four hours grew to seven on the Thursday and their hopes were rising that they would be in reasonable shape to defend their European title. However there were only eleven days left before the start of the championships in Dortmund.

Then on the Friday they again fell on the first lift—not as catastrophically as before, but decisively as it turned out. This fall hurt Jayne's pride more than her body and they were able to continue with the practice, but they were both shaken by the experience, particularly Chris. He seemed the more nervous of the two attempting the lift again 'because I did not know until I turned whether I was going to fall or not. It was kind of make or break. I turned on two feet, but turning from one direction to another you have to be on one foot at one point.' The fall was less dramatic than the previous one, but Betty Callaway, who was teaching another couple on the rink at the time, saw it happen this time and persuaded them to change the programme. They agreed—with some misgivings because it seemed that they had been defeated and they are too competitive to take kindly to that.

Devising a new lift took time and they had to switch to the ballet-room before the inspiration came. Back on the ice they showed it to Mrs Callaway and she declared it to be better than the one it had

Practising painting on the clown's faces for their *Barnum* programme in the ballet-room at Oberstdorf in preparation for the world championships at Helsinki, 1983 (*All-Sport Photographic*)

replaced. It now seemed all systems were go but over the weekend there was a final setback. Jayne's arm stiffened and by the Monday they could no longer even do the compulsories, with the new arm movements they had introduced. Their despair was rubbed home by the sight of two German couples and one from France, all Dortmund-bound, firing on all cyclinders.

It was time to confess to each other what they had already decided in their own minds, that Dortmund was out. They gave it one more token shot the following day but Jayne had to leave the ice early, declaring that she would not skate again until she could skate properly. The meeting in Betty Callaway's room at which they decided to withdraw from the European championships was a formality. The next day they accepted an invitation to spend a few days in Munich with a friend, Clarissa von Lerchenfeld, whose family had been generous benefactors in so many ways for a year and more. Thus they were safely out of reach when the stunning news spread that they could not defend their European title.

By now their relationship had become strained through sheer frustration. Chris, spared the pain and poultices, was bored nearly out of his mind and his irritation rubbed off on Jayne. The decision not to skate in Dortmund lifted a weight from their minds and the three days in Munich—devoted to shopping, dinner with friends and the cinema—was the best kind of therapy for their morale. The total rapport that characterises their relationship returned.

Back in Oberstdorf the following weekend, their spirits were further raised by an invitation from Baroness von Lerchenfeld to a Bavarian evening in a plush Alpine restaurant which required them to dress in local costume—Jayne in a fetching *dirndl* dress and Chris a Bavarian jacket. By all accounts they looked sensational. But before that, full of the zest of convalescence, they had gone for a run, undaunted by the snow piled up in the streets.

Jayne resumed treatment at the hospital, with sauna and swimming at the complex, and suddenly the arm felt a lot easier. By the time I visited them on the day after the European championships finished, Chris mused how the trip to Munich seemed such a long way off, because they had 'gone from doing virtually nothing to virtually everything in one week'. They excluded the more demanding movements only as a security measure against a possible relapse.

Even so, a first view of Jayne that Sunday was alarming. She was swathed in blankets with only a head and arm exposed, the arm released only to spare her a possible attack of claustrophobia. When, in time, she emerged, after manipulative and electrical treatment, she seemed as good as new. She displayed the two packs applied to her right shoulder and the muscle below the shoulder, rather like slabs of black toffee moulded to the contours of her body by the heat. They were of fango, a therapeutic black earth, supplemented by certain minerals.

There followed a test for both of them on a cycling machine equipped with computer and a monitor clipped to the ear. This gave a highly encouraging reading of heart and pulse for Jayne, a disappointing one for Chris since he marginally failed to reach the superman register. 'I told you he hates being second,' Jayne chuckled. The biggest threat to her well-being now seemed to be the wearing of fashionable city shoes on treacherous ice when they went out to dinner again at the Lerchenfeld's.

They had not watched the European championships on television—because they preferred to remain in ignorance of what their rivals were doing and because it was a painful remainder of what-might-have-been. It was, as Chris said, 'as though it had never

happened'. They were aware from other people's remarks, however, that they had been missed. Yet Jayne struck a note of sympathy for Bestemianova and Bukin. 'I've no doubt,' she said, 'that people will have asked them if they thought they would have won had Torvill and Dean been there. That can't have been very nice for them.' Torvill and Dean seemed of a mind to spare them that unpleasant experience at Helsinki.

They took the precaution of not jumping the gun this time, having learnt the lesson of the second accident following so soon after the first. Not until two weeks or so before leaving for Helsinki did they start doing complete run-throughs of the free dance and rock 'n' roll. 'We weren't going to be silly and hurry it,' Chris says, 'and maybe damage something again. We had more time [having missed the week in Dortmund and the week's rest that would have followed] and we did not rush into things, just to be able to say we could do it. We let the arm and shoulder build up.' Sometimes Jayne would take a sauna between training periods to ease the ache.

They told a fib on their arrival in Helsinki. All was now well and Jayne was fighting fit again, they said. Fighting she may have been—for there are great depths of courage in that small frame—but her fitness was such that away from prying eyes she had to be strapped up every day throughout the competition to support the right shoulder and a large area of the back. Then she had to be unstrapped every night, a painful experience, however tenderly Chris plied the scissors and cleansing fluid. The skin was sore but the doctor at Oberstdorf told her that it would have been worse, if it had not been in such good condition to start with. It was a tiny deception, designed to divert attention from the injury and forestall any imagined weakness in their skating.

Another secret had to be kept, for fluid had begun to gather on Chris's right knee two days before they left their training quarters in Oberstdorf for Helsinki, eight days before the competition started. He had not felt any pain, but the fear remained that the knee might seize up altogether. Twice a day in Helsinki he had to have electric treatment and at night the knee was heavily bandaged. After every training period he had crushed ice brought to his room and massaged the knee. He also did exercises specially designed to dispel the fluid. By the end of the week it had almost subsided and did not, happily, impair his skating.

On the eve of the world championships in Helsinki they drew the

Dr Hans Rohde (centre) and the physiotherapist, Klaus Behke, testing Jayne's fitness in the orthopaedic clinic at Oberstdorf after her accident in January, 1983 (*All-Sport Photographic*)

lucky number—thirteen. This gave them good starting positions in the compulsories. They would skate third in the quickstep after resurfacing of ice and first in the Argentine tango, the dances most likely to cause concern over rutted ice. They skated seventh in the second dance, the Ravensburger waltz, but that would cause them no problem, Jayne insisted. Leaving nothing to chance they had, in any case, taken precautions against this particular quirk of fate by 'skating the ruts' in practice.

When the competition began, with the quickstep, they immediately built up a big lead with an average mark of 5.8. This was nothing exceptional for them, but they had skated well and were on average a quarter of a mark ahead of the next couple, Blumberg and Seibert. Chris was perfectly satisfied, recognising that the judges 'always take a little time to find their bearings at the start of a championship'.

They are not sure that the Ravensburger was better skated—there was nothing wrong with the quickstep—but it was better marked. They introduced variations in each of the three sequences and Jayne performed the twizzles, a rotation characteristic of ice dance, with the free foot in front and the knee slightly raised. 'Some people might find it harder that way,' she explains, 'but it comes just as easy to me and I think it's more effective, prettier.' Yet again they were breaking new ground, even in the compulsories.

By now they were virtually out of sight of the rest so far as the first section of the competition was concerned, but they rounded it off with an exquisite Argentine tango, 'the best compulsory we've ever done', Chris thought. The judges agreed because they gave them an unprecedented row of nine 5.9s. At least three judges confessed in confidence afterwards that had the British couple skated towards the end of the field instead of at the very start they would have awarded them a 6.0. Their forbearance left Chris and Jayne with a second burning ambition, a compulsory 6.0. The first, of course, is the Olympic gold medal at Sarajevo next February. 'I didn't tell Jayne, but I consciously went out there to skate a 6.0 to try to stimulate myself,' says Chris. Jayne 'just wanted to give everything'.

There was another novel touch about the tango. Three tunes are used for each of the compulsory dances, repeated to the point where even ardent followers of ice dance are driven to distraction over a period of up to two hours. All three pieces of music appropriate to the dance are played in each warm-up for skaters to attune themselves to the music they will skate to, but as Chris and Jayne were skating first they elected to skip the third tune. That left two tunes and Jayne hit upon the idea that, as they would have virtually clean ice on which to skate, it would be better to practise only once from the correct end of the rink, so that they would lay down one tracing to follow and not provide further ruts for themselves. For the other warm-up dance, in fact the first, they began at the wrong end of the rink. Other skaters would trace their patterns in the warm-up, but they would vary and create no difficulty. Jayne was not aware that any other skaters had warmed up in this way before. 'We never had,' she said. 'It was just an opportunity provided by the draw. **,**

They had now set a new standard for compulsory dances, but you would never detect it from the tone of the subsequent conversation over coffee a few days later in Helsinki's Inter-Continental Hotel. Apart from Chris's confession that he had sought a 6.0, everything seemed so run-of-the-mill. There was nothing to suggest that here, as in other areas of ice dance, they were fashion-setters—flouters of convention not for its own sake, but in an attempt to open up new fields of individual expression. As a by-product, they were almost certainly instilling in their nearest challengers a sense of clear inferiority. The tango in particular, skated to 'Jealousy', arguably the best tango song ever written, was a demonstration of extraordinary elegance, charm and characterisation. They conveyed such an impression of haughty arrogance that it stood out in stark contrast against the gaiety of the quickstep and waltz that had preceded it. Can it possibly be better done?

The arrival of Michael Crawford on the Monday had been a blessing. They had been in Helsinki four days and that already was about two days too long, because they had arrived with a thirst for the battle after having had to surrender their European title by default at Dortmund. Michael lifted their spirits immediately and carried them into the compulsories with their morale on the bubble. Mostly, he was Chris's companion in the evenings, since Jayne had various chores to attend to and often dined in her room. Chris:

❛ Michael was good for us because he put us in the right mood, like on the morning of the OSP practice, for instance. That was held in the cold rink half an hour away in the sticks and, though all the judges were there, it didn't seem like a full rehearsal. Michael put our doubts at rest. We'd done well, he assured us, but we'd lit only the 60-watt bulb, building up to the real thing. That evening we would light up the 100-watt bulb in centre ring. He makes you feel that everything you do is absolutely right for what you are trying to achieve. He was a very positive influence. But we must not play down Betty's part. She has been there all the time, the rock for us to lean on. And she showed no resentment at the attention that Michael received by people who lacked the sensitivity to understand her special position in our world.

The day after Michael arrived we had free dance practice in the evening and we were the only ones on the ice. That gave us an ideal opportunity to show him the programme. He had not seen it before, except in the British on television, and he made two points that were really useful. As Betty will tell you, when you see a programme regularly day in and day out you can drift into bad habits without it being obvious except to a fresh pair of eyes. Michael was able to draw on his theatre experience. From time to time, he told us, he has his performance put on video so that he can search out any flaws. It may feel exactly the same, but you are economising all the time. You draw into yourself and you need to see yourself periodically to discover whether you need to extend and push. With *Barnum* I felt that we improved with every run-through. If it were possible to compare the first run-through when we arrived with the actual free dance on the final afternoon, you would see a big improvement. *9*

The OSP embraced marvellously intentive contortions—all ingeniously fitted into the thumping beat of the Andrew Lloyd Webber variation on a Paganini theme—and achieved new levels of originality. Just as the music belonged to another world to the rest, so the performance was in a different league, too. It was even more intricate than the original rock 'n' roll presented at Nottingham the previous November, with one or two little flat parts removed and a breathtaking opening where Jayne leans backwards almost on to the ice, supported merely by her partner's right hand, spinning her head as she rises rather like the clown with a ball in *Barnum*. 'The lower Jayne goes the more interesting the move looks,' Chris explained. 'The only difficulty is that if Jayne breaks her hips my hand slips off the back of the neck and she's on the deck. She's had some headaches in practice.'

There was one hair-raising moment in the first sequence when a look of alarm flashed momentarily between the two. They were performing the lateral twist, 'the neck thing' as they came to call it with little respect for elegance of terminology. The move has Chris unwrapping Jayne like a roll of carpet and, as she spun into position with her right hand behind her back, her skirt billowed out and its material floated between the two hands as Chris took his grip. 'I saw dread in her eyes,' Chris reported later. Jayne says, 'He looked as if he was thinking "This is a fine mess you've got me into".'

They knew from experience in training what serious options lay ahead. As Chris hauled his partner up from a now horizontal

The exciting rock 'n' roll OSP in the world championships at Helsinki, March 1983 (*All-Sport Photographic*)

position, a firm grip would be likely to rip the skirt as it had done in practice; or the skirt might hold and they would come to an abrupt halt as had also happened before. With luck, though, the material—a synthetic satin—might slide from between their hands. Fortunately, they were able to release the grip a little, retaining hold mainly through the fingers and so allow the skirt to slip free.

They had been no more than a inch or two from possible disaster. Even so, there was insufficient purchase for Chris's left hand on Jayne's right for the pull to the vertical and the loss of momentum prevented them from flowing into the next move as readily as they would have liked. That, however, was a small price to pay compared with what might have been. For the two remaining sequences of the dance, Jayne took the precaution of placing her right hand higher up her back and spinning less freely into position so that Chris was able to gain a clean hold.

Their dice with disaster went unnoticed to all save a few eagle-eyed spectators seated close to Lawrence Demmy, the referee, and they registered the highest marks ever for an OSP, including seven 6.0s, five more than in the British version and one more than Copenhagen's 'Summertime' blues. Those in the know might have detected signs that Jayne's shoulder was still causing concern, for the material of the tee-shirt she wore for the OSP—in fact the top half of a white leotard—was thin enough for the strapping to show through, supposing you could get close enough and were sufficiently inquisitive. The wisp of red scarf around her neck offered a small measure of camouflage, however, and the secret remained intact, so far as the press was concerned at any rate.

The rock 'n' roll, which might have been designed specifically to test ailing shoulders, gave encouragement since Jayne had felt no twinges, either in the 'neck thing' or in the move where Jayne sweeps a circle with her right leg, moving backwards. For that, she takes her weight with both arms twisted behind her partner's back. They came off the ice feeling elated. 'We could judge from the audience reaction how well we'd done,' Chris said, 'how it looked to other people, because all the way round the rink they were clapping. Perhaps there were more British there that day. We felt that we'd entertained them and the marks would come along with that.' In fact there were few British spectators in Helsinki and Chris clearly did not appreciate the affection the Finns felt for him and Jayne. The banner bearing the device 'JAYNE + CHRIS' that greeted them every time they took the ice was hoisted by their Oberstdorf friends and benefactors, Baroness and Clarissa von Lerchenfeld.

Their marks included a 6.0 for composition (technical merit) and six 6.0s for presentation (artistic impression). The remaining marks

The rock 'n' roll put heavy strains on Jayne's injured shoulder which, contrary to their announcement for public consumption, was not fully cured at Helsinki; the strapping down Jayne's right side may just be discerned under the T-shirt (*Colorsport*)

A formal pose with Lawrence Demmy at the British Embassy, Helsinki, March 1983 (*Ice & Roller Skate Magazine*)

were all 5.9, including two from an obviously impartial British judge, Roy Mason. The Swiss judge, Jürg Wilhelm, seemed to be in their thrall. Apart from two 6.0s here, he had already given 5.9s for all three compulsories and would give another 6.0, plus a 5.9, for their free dance. Put together, that represents a remarkably comprehensive seal of approval.

The interval between Thursday's OSP and Saturday's free was 'a long day', Chris recalls. A visit to the shops with Michael Crawford and a starring appearance at the British Embassy, to publicise the case for holding the 1986 world championships in Birmingham, helped to eke away the hours, but at their pitch of activity it seemed a long time to pass without any exercise. They went straight from the Embassy to the rink for a final run-through of the free. They had skipped the practice on Thursday after the OSP, so it had been two whole days—and the way Chris says it, it sounds like an eternity—since they last rehearsed *Barnum*. It was not the best practice they had done but 'right for Friday', Chris explains, leaving them something more to reach for the following day. After breakfast in Jayne's room, the Saturday morning drifted by with no sign of nerves on their part. They were, Jayne says, 'absolutely keyed up to turn it on'. It was important now to time their departure for the rink right. Chris:

❝It's a funny thing, you can go to the rink too early and get past the point of wanting to skate, or you can go too late and not be keyed up enough. There's a right time for us, about an hour and a half before we are due to go on. Before we left that Saturday, Betty told me that, unexpectedly, our mothers were being flown out by the local newspaper and would arrive during the competition. Should we tell Jayne? At first I said no, but then I realised that if she happened to see her mum in the crowd it might distract her, break her concentration. When we did decide to tell Jayne it gave her a big lift. ❞

Their luck with the draw had held. They were to skate third in the last group, followed by Bestemianova and Bukin, then lying third, and Blumberg and Seibert, in second place. There would not be that much time after the warm-up for them to fret and they were in a position to exert psychological pressure on their main rivals if they did turn it on. Back in her dressing-room, Jayne says, 'I had that feeling of expectancy again among the whole audience, of the atmosphere building up for us nicely. I felt that people out there were eagerly waiting to see *Barnum*, to see what we could do with a theme like that.'

174

Neither of them, they say, felt at all nervous. Betty had elephants rather than butterflies in her stomach, she said; Michael had run out of fingernails and begun to attack the fingers themselves; millions of viewers at home, one later learnt, were reaching for the valium bottle to quell throbbing hearts. 'We were just bursting to get going,' Chris recalls. 'What little tension we felt vanished with the first note of the music, just as athletes feel better when the pistol goes and they are away.' Looking back, Jayne says:

❝You know from that first note how you feel, and we felt great. We became so lost in the performance that neither of us, forty-eight hours later, could really remember much about it. We just felt it was our best skating performance since we came together eight years ago, even better than *Mack and Mabel*. It may seem contradictory to say on the one hand that we can't remember it and on the other that it was our best skating performance, but that was the feeling we got from it. ❞

Michael Crawford, Chris adds, had a lovely expression that typified it all:

❝As you're getting to the end of a play, he said, you're coming home. That thought came to me twice, first before we went on, and secondly when the last tune began. I began to get a glow of achievement. We were coming home at the end of a long and troubled road. We'd been given four minutes on the line, on this particular day, at this particular time, to show what we were made of. ❞

At the end, the applause came thundering in from all sides of the only full house of the week — such is the present appeal of ice dance—and Chris and Jayne performed the ceremonial ritual in the centre of the ice—a studied bow from him, a deep sustained curtsey from her, first to the side occupied by the judges, and then to the other three sides in turn. Flowers and other gifts came raining in and by the time they had taken their places before the television camera the marks for technical merit had already been displayed—nine 5.9s.
There was a few moments' pause, during which 'I felt that the crowd was holding its breath', Jayne recalls, 'expecting perhaps some 6.0s for the second mark'. *Some* 6.0s? There was, for the first time in any form of ice skating, nothing *but* 6.0s as the scores of the nine judges flashed up: 6.0, 6.0, 6.0, 6.0, 6.0, 6.0, 6.0, 6.0, 6.0. 'Six point zero, six point zero...' the announcer intoned with delicious monotony in both Finnish and English. Jayne's face vanished behind

a cavernous smile; Betty Callaway, so unemotional in the ordinary way, positively glowed; Michael Crawford punched the air in the manner of a footballer who has just scored the winning goal in the Cup Final; Chris's expression was more one of deep satisfaction. He explained later:

❝Everyone places so much emphasis on the marks, but my thrill was when we went boom, boom at the finish, and the crowds stood to us. That was the biggest point. They were fabulous. OK, we were thrilled with the marks, too, but less so than the moment when we finished the programme. I felt a surge of emotion, because we had put so much into *Barnum* and had now brought it home in style. It did not come good by itself. It came good because we made it. That was the thing. We made it happen, and against the odds. Some people thought that we might be under par, but if anything we were stronger than ever. ❞

Some idea of the dominance they achieved in Helsinki may be

Chris and Jayne are themselves hit for six by the marks for artistic impression for the *Barnum* free dance at the world championships, Helsinki, 1983; all nine judges gave them the maximum mark of 6.0, a record for any form of international ice skating (*Lehtikuva Oy*)

World champions for the third time, Chris and Jayne—flanked by Natalya Bestemianova and Andrei Bukin (left) and Judy Blumberg and Michael Seibert—acknowledge the Helsinki spectators' applause (*Lehtikuva Oy*)

gleaned from a comparison of their average marks with those of the other two medal winners:

	Torvill Dean	Bestemianova Bukin	Blumberg Seibert
Compulsory dances	5.856	5.585	5.604
Original set pattern	5.939	5.628	5.744
Free dance	5.950	5.789	5.772
Overall	5.906	5.656	5.692

There was, alas, one drawback with *Barnum*. One needed to be in three or four different places round the arena fully to appreciate it. Even sitting behind the referee, as I was at the invitation of the Lerchenfelds, I could not take it all in. That was, though, easily the best vantage point and it was a serious lapse on the part of the television authorities not to have a camera perched there—not merely for *Barnum*, of course, but for all the skating in the main rink that week.

Chris and Jayne have gradually come to terms with the ordeal by interview. Here Jayne faces an Helsinki microphone with serenity and Michael Crawford's obvious approval (*Eileen Langsdale/Supersport Photographs*)

Viewers at home could not begin to appreciate the painting of smiles on the clowns' faces, or the look of horror on Jayne's face as she began to topple from the tightrope. The juggling would have been lost on spectators sitting to the right of the judges, and those at the other end must have been baffled to know how Jayne suddenly appeared head first and upside down through Chris's legs at one spectacular point. They could all, however, marvel at the sleight of foot as the champions proceeded down the length of the rink with Jayne's right leg swinging under Chris's left, at Jayne's windmilling simulation of drums being rolled into the circus ring, and to the impression of trombone-playing as they were invited to 'Come

One of the more remarkable circus tricks during their *Barnum* programme; Jayne dives head-first and upside-down between Chris's legs and still recovers her position on the ice to hit the precise note of the music—a masterpiece not only of acrobatics but also of timing (*Lehtikuva Oy*)

follow the band'. It was all embellished by typically bizarre clownish movements and topped off by a sensational back somersault by Jayne, helped on her way by Chris's head thrust between the legs, one of the many refinements on their Nottingham programme.

Amid all the subsequent expressions of adulation, it must be noted that some questions were asked as to whether *Barnum*, brilliantly conceived and executed though it was, was true ice dancing. However, as Lawrence Demmy points out, the ISU rules were revised in May 1982 allowing greater latitude. Although a number of the elements in *Barnum* might not be allowed in the normal course of events, it had to be recognised that it had a circus theme and 'characterisation of the music' gave a certain licence. The nine exacting international judges were, after all, absolutely unanimous. Here is their full set of marks:

	1	2	3	4	5	6	7	8	9
COMPULSORY DANCES									
Quickstep	5.8	5.9	5.7	5.8	5.8	5.8	5.7	5.8	5.9
Ravensburger Waltz	5.9	5.9	5.8	5.9	5.9	5.9	5.8	5.9	5.8
Argentine Tango	5.9	5.9	5.9	5.9	5.9	5.9	5.9	5.9	5.9
Total points	17.6	17.7	17.4	17.6	17.6	17.6	17.4	17.6	17.6
Placing	1	1	1	1	1	1	1	1	1
ORIGINAL SET PATTERN DANCE									
Composition	5.9	6.0	5.9	5.9	5.9	5.9	5.9	5.9	5.9
Presentation	6.0	6.0	6.0	6.0	6.0	5.9	5.9	6.0	5.9
Total points	11.9	12.0	11.9	11.9	11.9	11.8	11.8	11.9	11.8
Placing	1	1	1	1	1	1	1	1	1
FREE DANCE									
Technical merit	5.9	5.9	5.9	5.9	5.9	5.9	5.9	5.9	5.9
Artistic impression	6.0	6.0	6.0	6.0	6.0	6.0	6.0	6.0	6.0
Total points	11.9	11.9	11.9	11.9	11.9	11.9	11.9	11.9	11.9
Placing	1	1	1	1	1	1	1	1	1

Judges: 1 Mrs Cia Bordogna (Italy)
2 Mr Jürg Wilhelm (Switzerland)
3 Mr Kazuo Ohashi (Japan)
4 Mrs Margaret Freepartner (USA)
5 Miss Ann Shaw (Canada)
6 Mrs Heide Maritcak (Austria)
7 Mr Igor Kabanov (USSR)
8 Mrs Katalin Alpern (Hungary)
9 Mr Roy Mason (GB)

World champions for the third time, Chris and Jayne performed their brilliant rumba exhibition at Helsinki by way of encore; their one superb lift fits perfectly into the expressive character of the dance (*Hs/Helsinki Kotilainen*)

'What next?', I asked Chris and Jayne when the excitement had died down a few days later and we got to contemplating the future. 'How much longer can you go on erecting new mountains to climb?' Chris peered absent-mindedly into his coffee cup. 'Perhaps,' he replied, 'we should skate "The impossible dream" next.' Before leaving Helsinki they learnt that the Nottingham City council had increased their grant by £4,000 in the final year leading up to the Olympics, and that moves were afoot to grant them the Freedom of the City. One began to wonder if any dream was impossible for them.

Bolero

The Olympic season loomed with a departure from convention more startling even than that which had launched *Mack and Mabel* and *Barnum* into breathtaking orbit. *Bolero*'s predecessors at least followed the custom of rhythmic variations in traditional observance of the rule that 'no programme may have more than three changes in the music'. Chris and Jayne now took the rule at its face value and concluded that there was no need to seek four rhythms, when three or two would meet the purpose. Or even one! It would mean, of course, that they would be unable to display their versatility of interpretation, but had they not already done that many times over? And might they not hope to add yet another dimension to the sport in artistic presentation? They were taking a risk, of course, but once the thought had entered their minds there was no shaking their resolve to do what they thought was right for them. Come the nine judges of the world in arms, they seemed to say in the manner of Hotspur, and we shall shock them.

As with *Barnum*, the idea of *Bolero* had entered their consciousness before the previous season had ended, but with this difference. Chris already had a circus theme in mind when he decided to cold-shoulder the Bolshoi in favour of the circus in March 1982. The seed of *Bolero* was sown by Chris even without his knowing in Feburary 1983, before in fact they went to Helsinki for the world championships of that year.

It is their practice to play music while they are training, whether merely warming up at the start of a training session or experimenting with various ideas. It was for this reason that Chris walked into a shop at Oberstdorf and walked out again with a cassette of Ravel's orchestral masterpiece, written for a new ballet conceived by Ida Rubinstein in 1929 and first performed at the Opéra, Paris, in November that year. Some may find its insistent repetition of two simple themes monotonous, unable to appreciate the subtlety of orchestration as it moves to a powerful crescendo. To Robert Stewart, who was to arrange the score for Chris and Jayne, it is 'a wonderful piece, amazing in colour. It's the way Ravel contrived the harmony in relation to the rhythm that makes it so brilliant.'

Stewart, a music teacher and church organist, was one of three men from unexpected quarters who produced the scores for both *Bolero* and the original set pattern dance that Chris and Jayne had to prepare for the paso doble. The first approach, through Michael

Crawford and his agent Michael Linnit, had been to Richard Hartley but Hartley had risen so sharply in the music world from a corner of the Tornadoes pop group a generation earlier that he was at that time writing the music for the 'Kennedy' television series. He had earlier made his name with the 'Rocky Horror Show'.

Thus it was that Stewart found the world ice-dance champions on his Wallington, Surrey, doormat accompanied by Michael Crawford one day in April 1983, and received a commission to write two scores, the second for the paso doble borrowed from Rimsky-Korsakov. They had considered a few strict-tempo paso dobles, but their restless search for something different rebelled against the conventional 4-4 beat. They were conscious of the ISU dismay at the possibility of having to sit through three hours of 'Viva España' and kindred pieces and its decision to accept a 6-8 rhythm. The question of whether or not a minute or so of Rimsky-Korsakov could be arranged in 6-8 time was put to Stewart, a man who had divested himself of the responsibilities of commercial music (Royal Philharmonic, West End musicals, Sadler's Wells and the Yvonne Arnaud Theatre, Guildford) for the quieter waters of teaching the boys of Wilson's School during the week and conducting a church choir at weekends. A first in music at Oxford was brought triumphantly to bear on this new exercise.

Not only that, but he also contrived to concertina $17\frac{1}{2}$ minutes of *Bolero* into $4\frac{1}{2}$ minutes for the free dance and yet retain something approaching the same overpowering crescendo effect. Jayne recalls that Stewart seemed confident about *Bolero* but nervous about the paso. 'We told him we like this bit, that bit, etc,' she explains, 'and he had to put them altogether. When you think about it, we were asking quite a lot of him and when we said we wanted to take the piano tracks to Oberstdorf a few days later he nearly fell through the floor.' Stewart found the paso a much more difficult exercise than *Bolero* 'because nobody seems to know what a paso doble really is. All the good references say it's not a paso doble at all, but a single step. We did it at a slightly slower tempo than it would normally go and I worked it out at one beat a second. That made an easy mathematical calculation for the number of bars I could use.'

Three months later Chris and Jayne flew home from Oberstdorf for a conspiratorial gathering in the house of Alan Hawkshaw, a former member of the Shadows pop group, who has since graduated—like Hartley and Stewart—to writing more substantial music, mostly for television. More than that, he has assembled in his house at Radlett, Hertfordshire, a bewildering mass of gadgetry at a

A dramatic moment from the hypnotic *Bolero* programme which sets new standards for artistic interpretation (*Bob Martin/Creative Sport*)

cost of some £200,000 which can produce almost every sound known to musical man. Hartley was to be responsible for producing the tapes in association with a technician on the console, while all three would take their turn at the keyboard of Hawkshaw's computerised synthesiser linked to a 24-track tape. For Hawkshaw, a little star-struck in the company of Chris and Jayne for all his show-business connections, 'it was like writing a song for Streisand'.

Hartley reckons that it would have needed a full orchestra to produce the sound that the world champions sought. In fact he needed only one live musician on alto sax, with Hawkshaw himself on snare drum, ordinarily a nightmare assignment over the full $17\frac{1}{2}$ minutes of *Bolero* because of the constant repetition. The effect of the other 70 or so musicians came from the keyboard. The advantage of the computer over an orchestra, Hartley explains, was that he was able to produce a 'dry sound, devoid of the blurring together that is part of the orchestral effect; that would have sounded too echoey in an ice rink'.

Chris and Jayne now returned to Oberstdorf with their complete tapes and began to adjust the programmes they had already prepared, with the British championship at Nottingham in November as their first target. They were committed to seven hours a day on the ice, made possibly only by the generosity of Marie-Therese Kreiselmeyer, the wife of the director of the Oberstdorf centre and herself a prominent ice-dance teacher. Not only was the second (mirror) rink often put at their exclusive disposal, but now they were locked away from prying eyes and ears, except for as much as could be seen through a few windows. The work load had to be increased because of the need to practise six compulsories instead of the usual three under a new ISU ruling.

Bolero took shape fairly rapidly. Chris:

❝ We had a lot of ideas and they came quickly. The hardest thing was disciplining ourselves to start slowly, something we'd never done before. And we were not sure people would appreciate what was necessary to skate that slowly, whether we'd be able to pull it off. We wanted to be able to create a certain shape. The first bit, just travelling down the rink and all the way back, was trying to create an impression of moving along, going to a destination. Then we had that bit when we started to wind and the whole pattern got bigger. We aimed to crescendo it, the same as the music, trying to be a little bit more spectacular every time something happens. It was difficult working out whether this move should go here or perhaps a little bit later. Also, some of the lines that were difficult may not have looked so difficult. You have to be interesting all the time. ❞

For their original set pattern paso doble Courtney Jones created a stunning outfit for Jayne, appropriate for her role as cape to Chris's dominating matador (*C. Erdil/Hungarian Studio of Publicity Photos*)

It was Jayne's turn to take up the theme of the paso doble:

❛ We started the paso when the *Bolero* was well on its way but not completely finished. By 'finished' I mean the steps, before we wanted to skate it out. We had a strong mind about what we wanted to do with the matador and cape. People wrote about that in various magazines, but nobody seemed to take it up. We didn't, of course, know what other people would do and, as we were curious to see what they were coming up with, we made a point of going to see the St Gervais competition in the summer as well as the Nebelhorn Trophy at Oberstdorf. There wasn't a hint that anyone was thinking along the same lines as we were. ❜

To start with, the paso doble came together with surprising speed, but there was to be an extraordinary hiccup before performing it in public in all its glittering glory at Nottingham. Courtney Jones's design for the cape was such that Jayne needed a special practice outfit modelled on similar lines to ensure that the holds they developed would still prove possible with the volume of flowing material that represented the cape. Jayne used a billowing red top for this purpose behind the locked doors of the second rink, but with the arrival of the complete orchestration on tape it was time to move out to the third rink which, like the first at Oberstdorf, is of the full size, 60 metres by 30. However, unwilling to give the game away, Jayne now wore a conventional practice costume, with depressing results. She continues:

❝ Now when I extended by arms it looked like nothing, with no cape draped from one set of fingertips to the other. People obviously didn't understand what we were doing and Chris began to get nervous. 'I'm going to change this bit or that bit,' he'd say every day, until the whole thing became a lot too busy, a lot too involved. We're not so cocksure of ourselves, you know, that we think everything we do is marvellous. We're deeply responsive to what people are thinking around us. Well, Courtney came out to Oberstdorf at this time and—here's a true friend for you—he said 'I think you've got it all wrong'. He was there only two days and in that time we changed so much that we came more or less back to the original. Isn't it a fascinating thing that the dress was actually dictating the dance? Since then we haven't touched it, except for small improvements here and there.

Chris, of course, is the star of this one. I've got to do my steps but slow things down so as to make it look as if he's pushing me and pulling me everywhere, doing everything. In a lot of places he doesn't even have any recognition of me because he's trying to convey the impression of looking over his shoulder for the bull. I have to play it deadpan with no more emotion than you would expect from something as inanimate as a cape. There had to be no eye contact between us. ❞

While all these things were taking shape abroad, here at home there were still more social engagements as the ripples of recognition for the British couple spread wider and wider. They were summoned once more to Downing Street to meet the Prime Minister and the Council House of Nottingham to receive the Freedom of the City. Jayne is the first woman to be so honoured and there was much aldermanic embarrassment that the official plaque, as revealed in a BBC television interview, carves her name with pride but imprecision as 'Jane Torvill'. With their help Jimmy Saville fixed it for five-

A sea of smiles reflects a city's pride as Chris and Jayne arrive at Nottingham's Council House to receive the Freedom of the City. Jayne is the first woman to be so honoured (*Nottingham Evening Post Photos*)

A charming interlude at Richmond in September 1983 when 5-year-old Hannah Bishop was allowed to fulfill her ambition to collect flowers for Chris and Jayne by courtesy of the BBC's 'Jim'll Fix It' programme (*Ice & Roller Skate Magazine*)

year-old Hannah Bishop, a little tot from Littlehampton, to collect their flowers from the ice at Richmond. The BBC Sports Review of the Year and the Sports Writers' Association continued to regard them as a team apart and command their attendance at official functions.

The new season opened with the British championship at Nottingham in November and that, in turn, opened with the newly-instituted draw for the compulsory dances. Group Two was chosen and in the third dance, a rumba, the champions introduced a lilting dip in each half sequence that may have so seduced Roy Mason as to elicit a 6.0 from him, thereby achieving one of their two remaining ambitions as amateur skaters. The other, the Olympic title, would have to wait on events.

The British championship was no contest, of course, so far as first place was concerned, but extraordinary public interest was aroused by this first chance to evaluate the new creations of Torvill and Dean, as they had now become known without the need for first names. Public appetite was fully assuaged by the OSP, with six 6.0s for presentation and 5.9 for every other mark. The free dance was less conclusive and a 'vox pop' conducted afterwards by the *Nottingham Evening Post* registered a number of preferences for *Barnum* the previous year. There was, perhaps, a tendency to compare like with unlike, since the *Barnum* that one remembered was the finished Helsinki performance. The Nottingham *Barnum* had been an inferior article, four months earlier in the season, containing a slip on the part of Jayne, seriously ill at ease in a dress that was unequal to the strain imposed on it. They had only one 6.0 then (and that surely an aberration) compared with six scored by *Bolero* a year later in a similar stage of evolution. The Nottingham championship told them something special about *Bolero*, as Chris explains:

❛ I felt we were so rehearsed that we were getting over the top with it, where we would do a run-through just to say we had done it, without putting any real feeling into it. We'd already started doing the full programme in August, which is exceptionally early. And you're not getting any real atmosphere with only Betty there. It's a difficult one to practise because it's very much a performing dance. We were running it through every day for two and half weeks, the whole thing, when we know now that we need a maximum of ten days to keep it fresh. ❜

The British championship provided one statistical footnote. The previous year, 1982, they had set a record of five successive victories and Jayne had become the first woman to bridge that span. Chris now surpassed Courtney Jones's five titles from 1956 to 1960, in the company of two partners.

Budapest, two months later, provided somewhat less than ideal conditions for the European championships. Chris and Jayne were at first inclined, drastically, not to use the second rink because not only was it below full size but there was a low ceiling that added to the claustrophobic effect. 'After a little while,' Chris noticed, 'your eye tended to drop because of the low ceiling. It made everything seem smaller than it already was.' They changed their minds about using the small rink in the end when they studied the practice schedule and discovered that they had only three periods on the main rink. Indeed, they hoped to turn the situation to their advantage. Jayne:

❲ In the end we did everything on the practice rink, partly to keep up our condition and partly to show it could be done. We were, if you like, exerting a little psychological pressure by showing we could do what we had to do whatever the conditions. It seemed a more professional approach. It may have been tactically unwise because undoubtedly the switch from one size of ice to another about four metres larger in both directions could possibly lower our performance. On the other hand we felt that any judges watching would appreciate the effort we were making to meet the conditions. ❳

As soon as the competition started Chris and Jayne knew they were among friends. They had only to put blade to ice to set off a volley of applause. On one occasion it was tinged with relief, for they arrived late for their warm-up under the erroneous impression that there was another couple to skate in the preceding group. Chris was not sure whether the warmth of their reception had anything to do with their connection with Regoeczy and Sallay and their having been to Budapest to train with the Hungarian champions in their earlier days. 'The Hungarians are a people of dance and sport,' he says, 'and we find that Eastern bloc countries are knowledgeable about sport. Perhaps, though, it helped that we were getting known.'

They began the championship with a superb rumba, with its highlight that dip on a deep right back outside edge which not only adds to the difficulty but also to the visual impact. They won the compulsory dance section easily, though there came two unexpected shots across their bows, the Russian judge giving them 5.7 for the Westminster waltz against a 5.8 for Bestemianova and Bukin and the French judge marking both couples 5.8. We were left to deduce that both judges were offended by the variation in one of the British holds. If that was a surprise, the same two judges' marks for the paso doble OSP the following day hit us like a thunderclap, for both placed the Russian couple first. Yet the British performance was so impressive that Miss Bestemianova herself later generously admitted: 'I could not free myself from the memory of it all day.' The full range of marks for the OSP, with Armelle Van Eybergen of France at No. 4 and Irina Absaliamova at No. 9, was:

	1	2	3	4	5	6	7	8	9
Torvill/Dean	5.9	5.9	5.9	5.8	5.9	5.9	5.9	5.8	5.6
	6.0	6.0	5.9	6.0	5.9	6.0	6.0	6.0	5.9
Bestemianova/Bukin	5.8	5.7	5.6	5.9	5.7	5.8	5.7	5.7	5.8
	5.8	5.9	5.7	5.9	5.8	5.8	5.8	5.8	5.8

I consulted both minority judges at the banquet that followed the championship and Mrs Van Eybergen explained that she took the view that the skid stop between sequences in the British paso infringed the rules, adding 'but I gave 6.0 for presentation'. When pressed, she admitted that there ought to have been more than 0.1 between the two couples in presentation in her opinion, but having given the Russians 5.9 she had no further latitude. Mrs Absaliamova, who proved to be a charming companion over a bottle of red wine, declined to comment, declaring that judges were not allowed to do so even after a competition is completed. From Laurence Demmy I discovered, however, that her objection was the same as Mrs Van Eybergen's, though she obviously took a much more serious view of the presumed British lapse. Demmy agreed with neither.

Looking back on the first two sections of the competition, both Chris and Jayne were bewildered. 'Everybody else though these were the best compulsories we'd ever done,' Jayne said, 'and we were marked down on the one we thought best of all. Everything came down to a technicality, about a hold in the Westminster waltz. It's a grey area and we don't think we were breaking any rules. Nor of course did seven other judges.' As for the OSP, Chris maintains:

❝We don't think we could have done it better, and it's the best OSP we've ever put together. Compared with Nottingham, it was bigger and better and so much faster over the ice because of the larger area to cover. Apart from that 5.6 from Mrs Absaliamova we were thrilled with the marks, with six 6.0s to add to our collection. We did not immediately appreciate what Mrs Van Eybergen had done, because we had not seen Bestemianova and Bukin skate and had no idea of their marks. ❞

Bolero was another triumphant occasion, with three marks of 6.0 for technical merit and eight of 6.0 for artistic impression. The

The 1983 European title recovered from Natalya Bestemianova and Andrei Bukin (left); Marina Klimova and Sergi Ponorenko have notice of a rising new Russian talent

European title, on loan to the Soviet Union after Jayne's injury the season before, was now back in Britain. Even the ranks of the Soviet Union and France could scarce forbear to cheer, for both judges gave 5.9 and 6.0. Even so, the dance was notable for a slip on the part of Chris, the only one I can recall in many years of Torvill and Dean-watching. At one passage he merely leans forward to take hold of Jayne's leg at a moment of no great tension and this time rocked too far on the blade, fractionally but conspicuously. Some British spectators felt they detected signs of nerves on Chris's part during *Bolero* and wondered if the pressure of gambling on a single rhythm had got to him, but that is not how he remembers it. Nor does Jayne. 'Had he been nervous,' she says, 'I would have been able to feel it. You can always tell, or at least we can.' How did they rate it among their various free programmes? Chris was the one to reply:

❛ We always say the one we're doing at the time is the one we like best. You've got to have faith in what you're doing. We had a nice feeling when we came off. As we finished there had been a second or so of silence and they then clapped, which is what we wanted to happen, to stir the emotions so that it would take a moment or two for people to respond. ❜

The statutory press conference after the championship was enlivened by a complaint of British malpractice by Tatiana Tarasova, trainer of Bestemianova and Bukin, who alleged that two of the British moves were illegal, since the man's hands rose above his shoulders. And anyway it was an exhibition not a free dance. This evoked a barbed response from the usually placid Betty Callaway. 'After 14 years,' she said, 'I'm delighted to discover that the Russians have found a rule book.' No doubt she recalled that Mrs Tarasova's prize pupils of the late seventies, Moiseyeva and Minenkov, had been held by some to have driven a troika and three through the rule book.

Were there British breaches? Laurence Demmy, a staunch defender of Moiseyeva and Minenkov in their time, now sprang to the support of his own compatriots. 'I'm not going to put a ruler across the shoulders to see if I can find a few inches of transgression,' he declared at the end of the competition. 'The spirit of the new rule is that there should be no leverage from above the shoulder and Chris certainly does not do that.'

Whatever the debate, Chris and Jayne beat Bestemianova and Bukin by nine judges to none, thereby adding substance to Miss Bestemianova's subsequent comment that 'it seems to be impossible to beat Torvill and Dean'. She would be given another chance a month later at Sarajevo.

Cheek to cheek

CHRISTOPHER DEAN BY JAYNE TORVILL

I can well imagine women's heads being turned by Chris. Mine was once, but I have known him so long now that he is almost a part of the furniture. That is not to say that I do not still recognise his good looks. With his blond hair, strong face, muscular frame and his way with good clothes, he is bound to draw lots of attention, but for the moment he has time only for his skating. He is very single-minded about that, if you will forgive the pun. When, occasionally, a girl has the idea of making a play for him he soon lets her get the message. He is not interested, not just now.

We were once very close, but that situation is hard to maintain when you work as intensely as we do at our skating. Quarrels are inevitable when you are doing something creative and a deep emotional attachment would be seriously at risk. Sometimes he hurts me with his gibes, nearly always on the ice under the pressure of inventing something new. I am not at my best first thing in the morning, and over the years that has meant any hour from about five to nine, whereas he is so thoroughly organised—probably because of his police training—that he is as lively as a cricket at the start of any day. He will sometimes start off with a kind of catechism, which I will try to answer as well as my drowsy state of mind will allow, something like this:

What have we got to consider today?
Free leg.
Yes, and..?
Hands.
Yes, yes and ...?
Back outside edge.
Yes, yes, yes. Brilliant!
Look, if I were perfect think how boring it would be for you.
Think what I could do if I had a decent partner.

Sometimes, but less often, I will be the one to lose my temper but I cannot match his brand of sarcasm. If Betty Callaway is with us she will step in to keep the peace. Where we are able to keep a civilised relationship is that we never carry our disagreements off the ice. We both realise that a certain amount of discord is inevitable, otherwise

Prepared once again for Astaire–Rogers, perfectly groomed and perfectly attuned to one another (*All-Sport Photographic*)

we would have to be paragons of virtue—which we are certainly not—or we would never attempt anything fraught with uncertainty. I mean, the man who never made a mistake never made anything.

It is rare for us to quarrel off the ice, sometimes only because I am a very tolerant person. For instance few people, I think, would stand for Chris's back-seat driving. He picks on me all the time, even when I am driving my own car for his benefit. When he drives it, on the other hand, I keep as quiet as a mouse, resigned to the fact that he is a tearaway and nothing I will say can change that. I would rather, though, that he tore away in somebody else's car. It would strike a nice balance, too, if just occasionally he had a go at another driver as slow and careful as me, or drove recklessly when he had some VIP as a passenger. It had to be me in the passenger seat one day at Oberstdorf when he roared round a corner and stopped only just in time to avoid an old lady finishing up on the bonnet, my bonnet.

I have, of course, a deep affection for him. I could not skate with him the way I do, pouring every emotion into it, if it were otherwise. And I could not spend practically every waking hour with him if it were otherwise. Apart from a week's holiday I took with my parents in Greece a few years ago, I have hardly spent a day without him from the time he came back from his police training at Dishforth in 1977. Travelling home from Oberstdorf for the first time on my own in 1982 for a recording session was an eerie experience. I missed him, and not only as someone to carry the bags.

Where does deep affection end and love start? I just do not know, but it is not a question that troubles me for the moment, not while we are training so hard for the Winter Olympics in 1984. For the moment, there is no room for an emotional commitment in my life, nor I am sure in Chris's. But I doubt if our partnership could survive if one or the other of us formed an attachment with somebody else off the ice. It is not simply that I would be consumed with black jealousy, which I expect I would; I just would not be able to give to any performance what I give to them all now. One of the secrets of our success, though it is hardly a secret, is the total commitment we make to each other on the ice. We could never have brought the same intensity of feeling to *Mack and Mabel* in our free dance of 1982, if we were not trying, both of us, to recapture the passion that existed between Mack Sennett and Mabel Normand.

The outstanding characteristic about Chris, I think, is his competitiveness. Whatever he is doing, dominoes or darts, bingo or beggar-your-neighbour, he has to win. He is fiercely determined not to be second best to anyone, anywhere. I am glad I have him as a partner and not an opponent. He throws himself whole-heartedly into any interest he develops. He was into photography once and he had to buy the best camera. He would not dream of starting off with an instamatic or anything like that. He had another craze for cycling and, of course, it had to be a flash racing machine, with all the gadgets. You would never see him riding a touring bike with a basket on the front and clips round his ankles.

He has to have the best, and *be* the best. We are both perfectionists, another important attribute, but in different ways. I am prepared to slog away at something until it comes right. Chris has much less patience and cannot understand when something we are trying for the first time—usually something quite complex and technically difficult—will not work straight away. Then his temper will show and he will give me a rough time. If not first thing in the morning, this will usually happen at the end of a hard day when we are both tired. I may feel irritable then, too, but I realise it is only because we need a break and I can keep calm. I am prepared to postpone what we are doing until the next day. Chris cannot. He is being beaten, and that is what he cannot take, so he will carry on with whatever is niggling him, like a dog with a tough old bone.

I think we are justified in taking a philosophical attitude to all this. We know that other couples have their spits, and the degree of acrimony is usually proportional to the standard they have achieved. Well, if it does not sound too immodest, we have reached a pretty high standard, so we have to accept a certain amount of disagreement as an occupational hazard. But let us not get this thing out of proportion. The time we spend quarrelling on the ice is infinitesimal compared with the total we are there, sometimes as much as six hours a day, six days a week, maybe seven. And apart from the odd little ribbing at other times we get along marvellously.

I sometimes think it is like a marriage really, apart from the fact that we spend the nights separately. We have much the same sense of humour, though his is a bit more weird than mine, like seeing a funny side of something that is basically rather sad. But on the other hand he is a very sensitive person underneath, easily hurt. He can be really happy one minute and, if something upsets him, absolutely flat the next. That was specially the case when he was under pressure with the police, but it happens much less frequently now. He is right, of course, to be annoyed by my bad timekeeping.

He is touchingly protective towards me. If there is any chance of my being knocked over on the ice he will swoop in and sweep me up like a little doll, he is that quick and strong. He would do it for anyone, of course, but I feel—no, I know—he will make a special effort for me and not only because without a partner he is a lost soul. He is a brilliant innovator on the ice and most of the pioneering things we have done are down to him. But it is hard for me to stand on one side and properly measure his genius (I do not think that is too strong a word) because we have grown up together and I have become used to his ways as we have gone along.

He is the dominant force when it comes to preparing programmes: whether he is such a dominant force in the actual performance I must leave others to judge. At first he certainly was, because he has always been an ice dancer, whereas to begin with I was a figure skater, either solo or pairs, sometimes both. I have worked hard to develop my ice personality in recent years, partly because of Chris's criticisms and I am satisfied that I have made some progress. How much, again, I leave others to decide. The point is that we have been successful as a couple and that is all that matters.

In a teaching role, we have given quite a bit of help to the Germans during our time training at Oberstdorf and it is usually Chris who gives them the ideas. I will offer an opinion about their quality and the timing. A couple of years ago he would drive too hard, insisting on would-be pupils repeating a move *ad nauseam* when it was clear to me that it would be better to give them a rest and try something else. More recently he has adopted a more

A putting green at Bournemouth provides a moment of relaxation, but Chris still leads the way while Jayne plays the willing and charming accomplice (*All-Sport Photographic*)

tolerant attitude, recognising that it is one thing to be a perfectionist himself, quite another to expect skaters who may not be of the required standard to master at once skills that are outside their immediate grasp.

You have to advance step by step, that is something we have learnt from Betty Callaway. It is hard enough for me when somebody is telling me to remember about half a dozen things at the same time. He now realises that it is pointless, perhaps even harmful, to try to force too much advice all at once on other people. As he mellows in that area he will be an outstanding instructor, because he understands so well the mechanics of skating and the importance of correct physical coordination.

He has become much more relaxed in his general attitude and socialises much more. He used to be embarrassingly shy, but year by year he has gained more self-confidence, especially after our second world title in 1982, and now he is at home in any company. After a championship, when I am ready for as early a night as I can get, he is prepared to sit up all hours chatting to anyone who will listen. His period with the police made him very self-sufficient and we sometimes experience a role reversal. He will wash and iron for me, not little things but something like a pair of trousers.

Many people were surprised to discover that Chris was no dab hand at ballroom dancing when we had to open the proceedings at the Sports Writers' Association party in 1981—Seb Coe having ducked out of being my partner—but it really is something quite different from ice dance. If he took the trouble I have no doubt he would pick it up quickly enough. I have shown him a few things, like the waltz and fox-trot, but he needs to practise it much more. On the other hand, he can see something in a musical, either in the theatre or the cinema, and pick it up straight away.

It has been an eye-opener to see how well he has come to terms with public speaking. Given his originally shy nature and his lack of opportunity, I would have expected him to be all 'ums' and 'ers'. When we were asked to do radio interviews in our early days he had little to say, left it all to me, and even then he was so tense that his breathing was uneven. Now I think he quite enjoys making little speeches. He is a little bit of a show-off off the ice, too, but not to excess.

I sometimes wonder what the future has in store for both of us. I am pretty sure I shall marry some day, but do not ask me who it will be. I have no idea myself, really. If we turn pro after the Olympics in 1984, actually after the world championships that follow, I cannot see it would work if one of us has formed an attachment elsewhere. But then, I cannot imagine getting married to Chris at the moment. Don't bet against it, though.

JAYNE TORVILL BY CHRISTOPHER DEAN

I have to see Jayne in a special light. Our skating is so all-absorbing that she has to be a friend and a partner. Other men may see her as the attractive charmer she is, but I have discovered from experience, we both have, that a romantic commitment would interfere with all we have worked for. That is in cold storage for us at the moment and neither of us will know what we shall find inside when the time comes for us to unlock the door. As she has already written, we were very close at one time. I think we fell in love and out again, but it is difficult to be sure because we were so young at the time. There was no sudden heartbreak, no discussion about it not being able to work. It is a strange relationship we have, a mystery to most people, including ourselves.

Any man would be happy to have her as a wife, once he accepted that she might not be content to be a cosy *hausfrau* with a brood of kids pattering round the kitchen floor. Somewhere in the course of our deliberations over this book she remarked on the prospect of telling her grandchildren about skiing round the Olympic cross-country course at Lake Placid in 1980. But children have to come before grandchildren in chronological order and she would have to come to terms with her comparative lack of domesticity.

Women do change, of course, and we all know of the most unlikely brides, all high heels and eyelashes, who have suddenly changed their character and revelled in childbearing and upbringing. You have to prise them out of the nursery. There is no reason why that should not happen to Jayne, but with culinary skills that fall short of boiling an egg and laundry skills that render her as likely to fly Concorde as operate a washing machine, she would have to undergo an abrupt change of personality. That is not to say it will not happen in good time. If and when it does I know she will cope well, because she is the sensible, level-headed type who would.

She is a super girl, totally honest and dependable (except in timekeeping) and absolutely unspoilt by the success she has had. She is the one who keeps the administrative wheels turning off the ice, attending to all the correspondence that has mounted with the years and keeping the books. Thanks to her, we can account for every

Literally cheek to cheek: many tender moments like this led Bernard Ford to comment on the obvious affection that exists between them—'you can't fake that sort of thing' he said (*All-Sport Photographic*)

penny we spend of the various grants we've received. She is the chancellor of our exchequer and when we are abroad I rarely have a pfennig or a franc in my pocket. Does that not sound ominously like a hen-pecked husband?

She looks after all the travel arrangements, with great efficiency except on one momentous occasion when we arrived at Montreal airport for the return journey to London after the 1978 world championships, only to discover that Jayne had thrown the air tickets away. Joan Wallis, the team leader, nearly threw a fit. I, on the other hand, carry the bags, open all the doors, do all the talking, go and fetch her tea and run her errands. Yet she still expects equal pay! She easily lapses into her little-girl role, to be placated by an ice cream or a soft toy. At such times I am a soft touch.

I suppose she looks small and vulnerable. I often treat her like that, throwing a screen round her when she needs protection. To hurt her is to hurt me and I would respond in the same way. But do not misjudge her. She has an enormous depth of character and would not be easily swayed from doing what she thought was right. There are some things about her, though, that get under my skin: her maddening inability for instance to keep any appointment, with the single, important exception of being on the ice at the right time. I am sure she does not mean to turn up late, but it always happens. Elizabeth Taylor is not in it. Since I am almost obsessional about meeting every engagement on the dot, if not well before, I find it hard to adjust to somebody who is so totally different.

It is the same with meals. I am quite happy to allow a social dinner date to proceed at a leisurely pace, since it is an occasion for social contact, but when, in the ordinary way, we could be back on the ice working it drives me crazy to watch her nibbling away at whatever is on her plate. For me, eating at this time is a necessary function and the sooner it is over the sooner I can get to do something worthwhile. But I have to sit and watch Jayne making a cack-handed attempt to deal, say, with a piece of steak. Her method—and it is not a pretty sight—is to trap the meat with her knife, held in the right hand against the left-hander's natural instinct, while she tears away at the meat with her fork. A pride of lions makes a tidier job of a stricken zebra.

She conducts herself impeccably in company (in private, too, for that matter) and can charm the judges off their bench, no doubt because of her natural modesty. Celebrity she may now be, but you would not see any change from the early days, except for the capacity to present herself in the best clothes and accessories. She believes, as I do, that now we are champions we have to behave like champions. She was never as shy as I was, but her retiring disposition allowed her at first to melt in a crowd. I would not say she has a riveting presence in a crowded room even now, but when she is drawn into the centre of attention, for a presentation or something like that, she is perfectly at ease. I think she is even beginning to enjoy the limelight.

As a skater she is the perfect partner, for me at least. Much of the originality of our programmes may come from me but that is only because Jayne makes it possible. She seems almost to float on the ice with a lovely, soft action and when I want her to go in a particular way she moves with no apparent effort on her part and little persuasion on mine. It just seems to happen, so much so that I tend to take her for granted. It is when I am trying to help another girl that I really realise my luck.

We seem, too, to have a telepathic understanding. Some people say that we are so perfectly tuned into the same wavelength that if one of us makes a mistake the other can instinctively cover it and it will go unnoticed. It may happen but I am not conscious of it. She is such a superlative technician that I know she will always be there, exactly where I want her, at precisely the split second. She is so sure-footed that I still cannot understand what went wrong at Dortmund during the world championships of 1980. She nearly fell twice in the OSP, an occurrence so shatteringly unlikely that I wonder whether or not I might have been to blame.

She used to be a bit withdrawn on the ice and lacked the extrovert attack that dancing needs, at least the OSP and free dance. Nobody would dream of saying that about her now. When I hear Lawrence Demmy talk of her sex appeal and Arnold Gerschwiler of her sizzling personality I marvel at the way she was able to adapt. It does not come easily for her to flaunt her hips as she does in our rumba, or declare her love so openly as she did in *Mack and Mabel*, or play the tragedienne as she did in our 'Summertime' blues. Even so, I am still not totally satisfied, slave driver that I am.

I used to say that she could portray only two moods, either happy or sad, and there are a thousand different emotions in between. 'Summertime' was comparatively easy to get into because it was on one level of suffering, but the melodramatic opening of *Mack and Mabel* was difficult because she had got to show anticipation, surprise, excitement, horror.

Sometimes I got mad with her. I used to say 'you've got to use your eyes, lift your eyebrows, show your teeth', or whatever. Our lack of any training in the theatre was a big disadvantage. You could see the difference with people like John Curry or Irina Moiseyeva. Irina always came over strongly with her facial expressions. She could do the Princess Diana bit to perfection by dropping her head, coyly lifting her pupils and showing the whites of her eyes. Jayne has got that well taped now in one of our exhibition numbers. She is a terrific worker and an avid learner.

Jayne will make a fine teacher some time if she ever decides to do that. She has much more patience than me and she has got the gift of being able to pass on her skill. Some people may feel that she would not be tough enough, but it is wrong to think that teachers should work their pupils aggressively hard. Certainly it is necessary sometimes to be firm and I am sure Jayne could be because she is the kind of person who weighs the pros and cons. And there is plenty of steel there, otherwise she would never have put up with me in my blacker moments.

Most people get the impression that I am quiet and I suppose I am in new company, but when we are working, or even at home, I can easily get aggressive. I rationalise my behaviour with the thought that it is probably necessary to put some bite in what we are trying to do, but it would be self-destructive if the other person were likely to explode so that we would fly apart. Sometimes, though, she does get mad with me and the odd mild expletive escapes. But that is unusual for her, because generally she is conventional in her behaviour—no bad language, no smoking (of course) and only the occasional glass of wine, and white at that. I've known her to be a little dizzy with drink, but never drunk.

I sometimes get to wondering what will happen after the 1983–4 season. At the moment we are cocooned in an amateur career that governs our every movement. But we shall be free agents, either individually or as a couple, in March 1984 and then we have to strike out in a different direction. Will it, perhaps, be two different directions? Ice dance couples, pair skaters too, no doubt, can suffer a terrible trauma when their competition days are over.

Courtney Jones has said that he and his partner, Doreen Denny, tactfully left alone by the rest of the company, were in tears after their last appearance together and Courtney suffered a nervous breakdown when Doreen went off to get married. Lawrence Demmy, another world champion, believes that Jayne and I have become so totally interdependent that separate survival would be extremely difficult. Judging by that, it almost seems that our destiny is out of our hands. It is frightening, really.

A position in the spotlight under a star in the ascendant symbolises, in a single frozen frame, the stature that Chris and Jayne have achieved in the world of ice skating (*All-Sport Photographic*)

Torvill and Dean milestones

1957 Jayne Torvill born, Nottingham (7 October)

1958 Christopher Colin Dean born, Nottingham (27 July)

1970 Jayne British junior pairs champion with Michael Hutchinson
Jayne 2nd British senior pairs championship with Michael Hutchinson

1971 Jayne British senior pairs champion with Michael Hutchinson

1972 Jayne 18th European pairs championship with Michael Hutchinson
Chris British primary dance champion with Sandra Elson
Jayne 2nd British senior pairs championship with Michael Hutchinson

1974 Chris British junior dance champion with Sandra Elson
Chris 6th British senior dance championship with Sandra Elson

1975 Chris and Jayne partners under Janet Sawbridge

1976 1st Sheffield Trophy
1st Northern championship
1st St Gervais
2nd Oberstdorf
4th British championship

1977 Chris posted to Dishforth
1st Oberstdorf
3rd British championship

1978 9th European championship, Strasbourg
11th World championship, Ottawa
Betty Callaway becomes trainer
1st John Davis Trophy
1st British championship (first 6.0)

1979 6th European championship, Zagreb
8th World championship, Vienna
2nd Rotary Watches competition, Richmond
1st British championship
2nd NHK competition, Tokyo

1980 4th European championship, Gothenburg
5th Olympic Games, Lake Placid
4th World championship, Dortmund
1st St Ivel competition, Richmond
Awarded MBE
1st British championship

British champions for the first time in 1978; Karen Barber and Nicky Slater were second and Kathryn Winter and Kim Spreyer third (*Ice & Roller Skate Magazine*)

1981 1st European championship, Innsbruck
      1st World championship, Hartford, Connecticut, USA
      1st St Ivel competition, Richmond
      1st British championship
1982 1st European championship, Lyons
      1st World championship, Copenhagen
      1st British championship
1983 Forced to withdraw from European championship, Dortmund, due to injury
      1st World championship, Helsinki
      1st British championship
1984 1st European championship, Budapest
      1st Olympic Games, Sarajevo

Acknowledgements

Although Christopher Dean and Jayne Torvill have a reputation for quiet withdrawal, especially where journalists are concerned, they were unexpectedly frank in the series of interviews that led to this publication. In order to flesh out the story, however, to give it perspective and balance, I have inevitably had to call on a number of other people at the heart of the skating scene.

First among them, of course, was Betty Callaway, without whom there might never have been a story to tell. She is the fount of all Torvill/Dean knowledge and has been unfailingly polite in response to a battery of requests for information. Roy Callaway, her former husband, was kind enough to turn the spotlight on her earlier years as a skater and teacher. I gladly join Chris and Jayne in the dedication.

I am also indebted to three men, Lawrence Demmy, Courtney Jones and Bernard Ford, who could offer comments from the standpoint of being former world champions themselves, to Pamela Davis, whose view was that of our most versatile and experienced judge in all forms of ice skating, and to Eileen Anderson and Joan Wallis, leaders of the British delegation at crucial moments and therefore battle-scarred administrative witnesses.

I could not, alas, give Janet Sawbridge—Chris and Jayne's first trainer—the chance to broaden the picture. In spite of widespread enquiries I was unable to trace her present whereabouts until the very day that the proofs reached me. By then it was too late, of course.

I am grateful to *The Sunday Times* for allowing us to reproduce their dance critic's fascinating foray into unfamiliar territory, to the *Daily Mail* and the *Nottingham Evening Post* for the provision of photographs, and to the National Skating Association for the use of their drawings of two compulsory dances. Mr Roy Yglesias also made a telling contribution with his historic photograph of the London Palladium in a little-known earlier existence as a skating arena.

Finally, a word of thanks to Michael Crawford, whose enthusiasm for the subject led to a pause in an interview at the Palladium while he explained the expertise of the juggler. No matter that the balls flew off into unexplored corners of his dressing-room. He did not miss a trick with the tape-recorder in his hand.

J.J.H.